Hoofprints

Sand

Library of Congress Control Number: 2001096886

ISBN 1-58150-074-2

Printed in Hong Kong
First Edition: April 2002

a division of
The Blood-Horse, Inc.
PUBLISHERS SINCE 1916

Hoofprints IN THE Sand

WILD HORSES OF THE ATLANTIC COAST

Bonnie S. Urquhart

EP
ECLIPSE
PRESS

Lexington, Kentucky

To Keith and Mark Bryan Scianna, my sons.
Of all the things I have done with my life,
bringing them into the world is the most significant.

Contents

Introduction

The wild filly watched me with gentle, intelligent eyes as I followed her movements with my telephoto lens. Pretending to ignore me, she strategically grazed closer and closer until she was only a few yards away. Then, unable to maintain her nonchalance any longer, she extended an outstretched neck and inquiring muzzle in my direction. She blew softly at me, filling flared nostrils with my scent. How strange. A human. And it's just sitting there.

Curiosity satisfied, she lifted her head and whickered softly to her herdmates. Silhouetted against the ocean sunset, she was a symbol of wildness, in tune with her own natural rhythms and in harmony with the fundamental forces that shape her world. In her momentary connection with me, she revived something within my own civilized soul that was as wild as she is.

When I first visited Cape Hatteras, North Carolina, I was amazed to learn of the presence of feral horses on several nearby coastal islands. It surprised me to learn that until recently feral horses and other livestock ranged on many East Coast barrier islands and today occupy islands off the coasts of Virginia, North Carolina, Maryland, and Georgia.

Fascinated, I looked in every gift shop and bookstore for information about the history and present situation of the herds. Which islands supported wild horses? Where did they come from? How did they live? What challenges did they face? What was their future? I was able to find several books (most of them for children) about individual populations, but not one that presented an overview of all the island herds. Local newspapers and regional magazines often wrote about them, but many of the details were inconsistent or appeared fanciful. When I consulted more arcane sources, I found errors, gaps, and contradictions. Frustrated by the lack of solid information, I became increasingly curious about their true origins and set about writing a book that would convey good solid information to other interested people.

I spent long hours in libraries and salt marshes separating fact from myth. I learned that each population of horses has its own character, its own history, and its own set of problems and concerns, and that in most cases these animals made a unique contribution to local history.

I learned that only hardy stock can thrive in a barrier-island environment. Summers are scorching and shade often scarce. Storms are frequent, winds intense, and sometimes the animals drown when stormy seas swallow the high ground. Enormous mosquitoes breed in the salt marshes, and biting flies are a bloodthirsty scourge, robbing each horse of up to five hundred cubic centimeters of blood per day!

I learned that most of these herds are controversial, and each has its own detractors and defenders. On the ferry to Cumberland Island, I sat beside two elderly bird-watchers, complete with wide-brimmed hats, binoculars, and Peterson guides. They were hoping to see a painted bunting on the island. When I told them I was writing about the feral horses, the ladies stiffened slightly. This was a sore subject for them.

"The horses shouldn't be there at all!" asserted one birder, a retired pediatrician. "They aren't native wildlife, and I don't understand why the Park Service allows them to remain!"

"But they are pretty!" her companion chimed in helpfully. The pediatrician raised an eyebrow at her friend, then conceded, "Yes, they are beautiful animals. But they have no business roaming on a national seashore."

Why is it that today's wild horse seems to have no niche and no real value? It seems that most people find beauty in horses, and, like me, thrill to the sight of a wild-born filly grazing on the dunes at sunset. Yet feral horses are also widely seen as pests, forced into inhospitable habitats or eradicated completely.

Accurate information is essential to wise management, but distorted pictures can be drawn from the statements of misinformed people and faulty research. Writers and readers alike often assume that anything that has appeared in print many times must be true and do not think to question the veracity of the information.

The behavior of horses in the wild state is complex and fascinating, and domestication alters the patterns so profoundly that many lifelong horse owners know little about the life of the wild horse. How do stallions establish dominance without coming to blows? How well do horses see? How intelligent are they? What do their vocalizations mean? How do they avoid incest? *Hoofprints in the Sand* seeks to provide some insight into how wild horses interact and to bring the physical nature of their lives closer to readers who will never observe a wild herd in the flesh.

In writing *Hoofprints*, I have made a sincere effort to set forth the facts as garnered from my own observations and from the most reliable resources. I hope I have fairly presented all sides of each issue so that readers might weigh the information and develop their own opinions.

As the technology-wielding dominant species, we are the guardians of wild creatures, and as such it is our duty to act in their best interest. We alter their destiny whether we act or choose to do nothing. We cannot allow raw emotion, nostalgia, politics, economic concerns, or public sentiment solely to decide the fate of these horses.

We can begin to deal wisely with them by understanding the facts and discovering how the threads of their existence relate to the rest of the tapestry. Only through understanding can we hope to make rational, educated decisions about the welfare of these unique animals.

Bonnie S. Urquhart
Hershey, Pennsylvania

Chapter 1 ⌘ WILD HORSES, FERAL HORSES

Wild horses have inhabited the barrier islands of the Atlantic Coast for centuries.

WILD HORSES, FERAL HORSES

Mystery and controversy surround the feral horses that live on our Atlantic coastal barrier islands. Where did they come from? Were their ancestors survivors of shipwreck or abandoned farm animals? It is clear that many of these herds have roamed freely for hundreds of years and are important to the cultural heritage of local residents. But their history is cloaked in legend and confusion, their needs sometimes conflict with those of other species, and their right to continued residency is disputed by everyone from real estate developers to biologists. Should they be allowed to remain?

Are these horses wild or feral? Native or exotic? Nuances of terminology affect management policies and influence the destiny of these herds. When we regard wild horses as wildlife, lawmakers and others are inclined to grant them protection. When we label them exotic, laws exclude them and public opinion supports their removal.

Should we consider a species wild only if its ances-

tors were untouched by human beings? This is a rare condition in today's world. Consider the dingoes of Australia. The dingo is a subspecies of the domestic dog that migrating Aborigines introduced from Asia about 5,000 to 15,000 years ago. The dingoes have lived in Australia for thousands of years and have a well-defined ecological niche. Are they wild animals? Of shorter tenure but just as biologically successful are the rabbits introduced to Australia in 1859 and the free-roaming hogs of Hawaii — as well as the North American mustangs and Australian Brumbie horses. How long must an animal persist in a new location before one can consider it an indigenous species?

Is an animal wild, no matter its ancestry, if it lives from birth to death independent of human influence? Or does wild mean unwilling to be fully domesticated, like the zebra? Przewalski horses do not allow themselves to be harness-broken or ridden, but they owe their continued existence to human intervention. If not for the actions of concerned people, the entire subspecies would be extinct. The current wild-living population has been re-established from zoo stock that was selectively bred for generations. Can they be considered wild?

These seemingly simple questions have complicated answers.

Furthermore, emotions are especially likely to cloud facts when horses are involved. Horses have been admired and romanticized for thousands of years. Even people who have never been close to a living horse appreciate its beauty and power on film and in art. The graceful, noble horse speaks to the heart and prompts enthusiastic public support in a way that hogs and goats do not.

Unlike most wild animals, free-roaming horses may not be hunted as game in the United States; unlike most domestic animals, they may not be slaughtered for meat. Ranchers complain that free-roaming horses compete with livestock for forage and often consider them a nuisance. Activists demand protection for horses and their habitat. If we cannot hunt them, eat them, ride them, or even get close enough to watch them, these horses are about as useful to humanity as cougars or wolves or other wild animals. If our minds and hearts accept them as wild animals, should we view them as exotics that have no right to the habitat that they have claimed for themselves?

Officially, free-roaming horses in the United States are considered feral, exotic, or non-native. The National Park Service, for example, defines *exotic* as "occurring in a given place as a result of direct or indirect, deliberate, or accidental actions by humans." *The American Heritage Dictionary* defines *feral* as either existing in a wild state or having returned to an untamed state from domestication. *Exotic* is sometimes defined as not present when European explorers first set foot on the North American continent.

But if Europeans had sailed to the New World 15,000 years earlier, they would have found vast herds of native horses, many different equine species that had evolved and thrived in North America over the past 55 million years. Events since 1492 make up the latest chapter in a long history of migrations, exterminations, and reintroductions that may have hopelessly blurred the boundaries between pony and horse, wild and feral, natural and artificial, Old World and New.

As the Pliocene drew to a close, prehistoric horses similar in size and build to today's Przewalski took advantage of a land bridge to the Old World, across what is now the Bering Strait. Some settled in Asian desert regions and evolved into asses and onagers. The horses that reached Africa gave rise to zebras and the small, hardy proto-Arabian horses. *Equus caballus* is the species that migrated through Asia and Europe and submitted to domestication.

Then suddenly, over a few thousand years, horses vanished from North America and South America.

TOM HALL

Przewalski's horse has been considered the last authentic wild horse.

Where horses numbered in the tens of millions, there were none for the first time in fifty-five million years. Eight thousand to ten thousand years ago, the last of them disappeared from the Americas. Woolly mammoths, dire wolves, saber-toothed cats, and North American camels became extinct in this same short time. There is no clear reason for their extinction, but excessive hunting by Paleo-Indians probably contributed.

Over the past two thousand years, more than one hundred additional mammal species have become extinct. In the last few centuries alone, humankind has exterminated the prolific, successful Tarpan horse, the Persian onager, the zebra-like quagga, and very nearly killed off the Przewalski as well. Meanwhile, other Old World horse populations continued to thrive. It is fortunate that horses had taken hold in Europe, Africa, and Asia, or they would have been forever lost to us.

Spanish Conquistadors reintroduced horses to the Americas in the 1500s. Their Iberian horses were bred for war and conquest and were renowned for intelligence, endurance, and tractability. After the Moors defeated Spain in 711, the Spanish realized that they needed a different kind of horse if they were to be successful in war. They crossed their own heavy draft stock with agile desert Barbs and Arabians, as well as Norse Dun Horses, to develop a deep-chested, short-legged, docile breed with great versatility. Known as Jennets or Jennettas, the horses of Andalusia and Seville were maneuverable in combat, yet enviably handsome and practical for farm work and general use. They fared well on poor forage, could tolerate extremes of weather, and could carry heavy riders long distances without fatigue.

By the time of Columbus' voyages, the Spanish equine population had been depleted by a series of wars, and it was difficult for the country to part with large numbers of horses to assist exploration. The ones that were shipped to the New World stood a fifty-fifty chance of surviving the voyage. As the death toll mounted, so many horse carcasses were pushed overboard that a section of the Atlantic was dubbed "the Horse Latitudes." (Becalmed ships would also lighten their loads and conserve precious water by throwing *live* horses overboard in these regions.) By the early 1500s Spain had established breeding ranches on Puerto Rico, Jamaica, Hispaniola, Cuba, and the mainland to provide mounts for expeditions and other purposes.

In addition to the Jennet foundation stock, breeders imported top-quality Barbs from North Africa to meet the demand for horses and add flavor to the genetic soup. New World horse breeders took pride in producing superior stock, and many made their fortunes selling horses to Conquistadors and others who sought to settle or exploit the New World. The islands were ideally suited to ranching, with no native predators, abundant forage, and a mild climate ideal not only for horses, but also for cattle and other livestock.

In 1519, Hernando Cortez set sail from Cuba to conquer Mexico with six hundred men and sixteen horses of chestnut, bay, pinto, sorrel, and roan. The native Aztecs of Mexico had never seen horses before and were initially terrified, believing this apparition to be supernatural in origin. Cortez was quick to use their wonder to his advantage.

Montezuma II, the ruler of the Aztecs, proclaimed Cortez the prophesied reincarnation of their god Quetzalcoatl and presented him with gold and silver gifts. But Cortez wanted wealth, not worship; conquest, not coexistence. Other tribes, tired of being ruled by the Aztecs, joined forces with Cortez, and the Aztecs fell. Cortez looted their gold and gemstones, and his success inspired further conquests.

By the seventeenth century, Indian tribes in present-day Texas and New Mexico — mostly Comanche and Apache — began to acquire horses. Initially, like their prehistoric ancestors, they used them as food. In the early 1600s, it

appears that the Spanish traded mares and breeding stock to northern Rio Grande and Plains tribes. In 1680, the successful revolt of the Pueblo people caused Spanish invaders to withdraw from the region, leaving thousands of their horses behind. Indian tribes traded and stole horses from one another, and more horses escaped to the wild from the loosely tended, unfenced herds.

Cortez repatriated the horse to its native North

The Peruvian Paso, a descendant of the Spanish Jennet horse.

American grazing grounds, the place where horses and their pre-equine ancestors thrived for more than fifty-five million years. How is it, then, that we do not consider them a native species?

The situation, of course, involves more than a simple change of residence. Horses were probably domesticated about six thousand years ago. Since that time, mankind has continually manipulated the genes of the original wild stock by selecting for body type, speed, disposition, and coloration. The Spanish horses brought by Cortez were nearly as far removed from wild *Equus* as a golden retriever is from a wolf.

Until recently, the Przewalski was considered the last authentic wild horse — but today's Przewalski is arguably no longer wild at all. While man was still living primitively in caves, *Equus przewalski* was proliferating across the plains of central Asia. It persisted tenaciously in the wild state until the 1960s. These animals were distinctively stocky and solid, displaying an upright mane, large heads, and dun coloration. The Przewalski has sixty-six chromosomes; one pair more than the domestic horse. Bred to the latter, Przewalskis produce robust, fertile hybrids with a chromosomal count of sixty-five.

Equus przewalski was adapted to life on the Siberian steppes. Ten thousand years ago, these horses were probably migratory animals, seasonally relocating by

The origins of today's free-roaming horses are likely to be diverse.

16

the thousands in the same fashion as reindeer. Eventually, mankind displaced the Przewalski from its preferred environment to the furnace-like Mongolian desert. They were actually able to thrive in this forbidding climate. But even in the Gobi wasteland, untamed horses were seen as a nuisance, consuming vegetation needed for domestic livestock and running off with mares in heat. Often stockmen shot them on sight. In 1968 the last documented Przewalski was observed in the wild. Zoos never acquired large numbers of the animals, so there was a small gene pool for captivity-bred horses. World War II further reduced the breeding population by destroying the entire herd at Askania Nova, a nature preserve in the Ukraine.

In 1973 only 206 Przewalskis existed worldwide, all in zoos. Twenty years later, the number had increased to one thousand. In 1993 a Dutch conservation foundation returned a herd to Mongolia and managed it there for a year while it adjusted to the challenging climate. In June of 1994, the foundation successfully freed nineteen horses where their ancestors had once ranged, and every year their numbers have increased.

These repatriated Przewalskis are the purebred descendants of wild horses captured from the wild and re-established into their natural environment. Then again, they are the result of generations of breedings carefully planned by zoos to give the few remaining survivors of the species the greatest possible genetic variability. There are no records of the Przewalski horse having ever been trained to ride or drive. (Other wild equine species, such as zebras and quaggas, have occasionally been saddle- or harness-broken.) Przewalski horses will submit to captivity and breed in zoos, but will not bend to the whims of a trainer. Are the captive horses domesticated? Are the released horses wild or feral?

The Tarpan Horse apparently roamed the vast forests and grasslands of Eastern Europe from prehistoric times. Expanding human cultures in the Ukraine and elsewhere domesticated a few Tarpans, ate others, and killed the rest as annoyances. In 1851 the Tarpan became extinct.

Recently researchers have tried to re-create the subspecies by mating horses thought to have a high percentage of Tarpan blood. Over time, they developed a primitive-looking, steel-gray dun that can be seen in zoos today. These animals look like Tarpans, but genetically cannot be considered to represent the original animal, for we do not even know its chromosomal count.

Each free-roaming horse alive in the world today has reached its present location and condition through the domestication of its ancestors or through selective breeding of captive stock. Serendipitously, features that gave the modern horse evolutionary advantages are precisely what facilitated domestication. The same dominance/submission social patterns that gave a horse

Today's Mustang is no longer purely of Spanish descent.

security within the hierarchy of his herd allowed him in many cases to submit willingly to human domination. Many wild species never became trusting or trustworthy despite long captive breeding, but horses were easily tamable, even after running feral for generations. They learned quickly and had indelible memories, were large enough to ride (most animals were not), and had a bone structure well suited to holding a saddle and bearing the weight of a rider. Few animals were as fast or could sustain speed over great distance. The horse could do this even while carrying a load.

Horse meat had long been a preferred food of early humans, but with domestication, other uses became apparent. Mares produced milk. Each horse could pull 300 pounds on a travois. A mounted warrior was far more intimidating and effective than one on foot and could travel great distances to attack. The domestication of the horse brought greater mobility, innovations in hunting and warfare, availability of leisure time, changes in social and economic values, and the sheer joy of racing the wind above the drumming of powerful hooves.

It probably did not take long for early breeders to choose stock with desirable traits such as speed, stamina, disposition, size, or eye-catching coloration. For the first time in history, horse phenotypes were determined more by human preferences than by environmental suitability and evolutionary advantages. Domestic horses gradually diverged from their wild cousins, and for

thousands of years humanity continued to manipulate equine genes, creating many diverse breeds.

Many researchers believe that if not for domestication, the horse would have become extinct. The range and numbers of wild horses contracted dramatically as the last ice age drew to a close. Then suddenly, around 6,000 B.C., horses resurged, becoming common wherever people were found. Similar population shifts occurred with other domestic species. The abundant aurochs were hunted to extinction after they gave rise to domestic cattle. Wolves were almost exterminated, but dogs persist. Wild sheep and goats are scarce, but domestic descendants flourish.

The Spanish Jennet horse that Cortez returned to the land of its ancestors does not exist today. D. Phillip Sponenberg, DVM, PhD, writes that through centuries of divergent selection, the horse currently in Spain is distinct from the Colonial Spanish Horse, and New World varieties are closer in type to the historic horse of the Golden Age of Spain than are the current horses in Iberia. There is great disagreement about which breed is its most direct descendant. Andalusians, Cerbat and Pryor Mountain Mustangs, Paso Finos, Peruvian Pasos, and the feral horses of Corolla, North Carolina, all descend from original Spanish stock, but have developed into unique breeds. In all cases, genetic experts suggest that blood has mixed and lines have diverged.

Equine geneticist E. Gus Cothran of the University of

Kentucky believes that the Pasos tend to be more like the Old World Iberian horses than other New World descendants of Iberian horses, but has not determined whether the Pasos are most like the original Jennet. Sponenberg points out that the old Spanish horse type was somewhat variable. This characteristic can be observed today in the strongly Spanish-blooded Lipizzaner breed. For centuries, Lipizzaners have been largely or wholly of Spanish blood, yet individuals show differences in type and conformation. It is likely the Jennets of the fifteenth and sixteenth centuries displayed a similar variability. Hope Ryden writes in her excellent book *America's Last Wild Horses* that Roman-nosed Barb-type and dished-faced Arabian-type individuals often can be found within the same homogeneous herd of Spanish-blooded Mustangs.

Breeders of Spanish horses selected body types that best suited their needs and aesthetics. Some types were refined until they became a distinct new breed, like today's Andalusians. Some were crossed with other breeds to create new lines. Thus the Jennet gave rise to countless other breeds.

In 1588 the English Navy defeated the Spanish Armada, a victory that eventually allowed England to colonize the New World, and soon the English seeded settlements all along the Eastern Seaboard. Many colonists were farmers, and they often bought livestock for their farms from Spanish ranches in the West Indies to avoid the hassle and losses of transatlantic shipping. Over time, American breeds like the Narragansett Pacer were developed for smooth travel over poor roads, and later Quarter Horses and Morgans became common along the East Coast.

In 1670 the English Parliament levied a tax on fences, which was unpopular with hard-working farmers. Coastal settlers in the American colonies cleverly circumvented this tax (and the cost of fencing, with or without tax) by putting their stock out to graze on barrier islands and peninsulas where the animals could range largely unfenced. Periodically, stockmen held roundups for the purpose of branding and collecting stock for sale or use. Otherwise, the herds were left largely to their own devices, migrating from island to island, grazing the marshes, and living the lives of wild horses. Sometimes livestock owners would die or move away, abandoning the herds to their wild existence.

Farther west, hardy Jennets were instrumental in the success of the Conquistadors, but with every Spanish settlement and expedition, more and more animals were lost to the wild. Within a century or two, feral North American Spanish Mustangs numbered in the millions and thrived in large numbers from Florida up through Oregon and Idaho into Canada. They enjoyed such amazing biological success that Charles Darwin, pondering the extinction of earlier horses, wrote in *Origin of Species*, "I was filled with astonishment; for, seeing that the horse, since its introduction by the Spaniards into South America, has run wild over the whole country and has increased in numbers at an unparalleled rate, I asked myself what could so recently have exterminated the former horse under conditions of life apparently so favorable."

Early Mustangs descended entirely from Spanish horses, but many other sources have contributed genes over the years. As civilization pressed westward, saddle horses, draft horses, and carriage horses escaped or were set free. Indians obtained horses from trappers, soldiers, farmers, and one another, only to have some of their own stock escape to the wild. Farmers who tried to wrest a living from the land often failed and returned east, abandoning their livestock. American horse breeds contributed subtle flavors to the genes of the Mustang. It is unlikely that any purely Spanish wild Mustangs remain, but most carry Spanish blood.

Feral horse populations remain on many barrier islands along the Atlantic coast, and their origins may be as diverse as those of the Mustang. The largest herds live on Sable Island, off the coast of Nova Scotia; Assateague Island, off Virginia and Maryland; the Currituck Banks of North Carolina; Ocracoke Island, North Carolina; Carrot Island and Shackleford Banks, North Carolina; and Cumberland Island, off the southern coast of Georgia. In addition, small unexpected pockets of feral horses exist in Missouri, Virginia, and other states. During research for this book, the author was told by locals about unpublicized populations on other small islands of coastal North Carolina.

While technically feral, all these free-roaming horses act wild, think wild, and have known nothing but a wild existence. Mankind has pushed them to the most inhospitable habitats, including deserts, swamps, mountain tops, and sandbars, where they usually manage to thrive, often reproducing at a rate that strains the local ecosystem.

Respected wildlife biologists such as Jay Kirkpatrick and Ron Keiper, impressed with the tenacity and prosperity of these horses, refer to them as wild despite their lineage. This book will use the terms wild and feral interchangeably.

Are barrier island equids horses or ponies? Some aficionados take offense at the use of one term or the other, but for many of the herds, either name is appropriate. By the horsemen's definition, any horse under 14.2 hands, or 58 inches at the withers, is a pony. Most of the island horses are fairly small and by this definition could be termed ponies, although in places like Corolla and Cumberland Island, many individuals surpass pony height.

There are genetic distinctions between ponies and horses, and biologists have determined that most of the island populations are genotypically horses. The harsh environment of barrier islands inhibits full

Though many are pony-sized, these barrier island equids genetically are horses.

BONNIE S. URQUHART

expression of genetic potential for stature, and many young foals removed from the islands outgrow their parents. In this century, local stockmen added Shetland-pony stallions to the Assateague herd to promote pinto coloration, leaving this group with a greater proportion of pony genes that contribute to their diminutive size. Even so, Chincoteague foals sold to the mainland at the Pony Penning festival often reach horse height at maturity.

Horses have been integral to human life for so long that our thinking about them tends to be either strictly utilitarian or uncritically emotional. Either can interfere with the study and management of wild equine populations in delicate environments. For thousands of years, up until the recent past, horses were instrumental to the progress of humanity, providing mankind with transportation, muscle power, companionship, and food. They have increased the efficiency of farming methods and fertilized crops with manure. Even cultures such as that of ancient Greece, which did not rely on horses as heavily for day-to-day survival, celebrated the aesthetic value of the horse in art.

Despite millennia of being exploited and venerated, wild horses occupy an ill-defined niche in today's world. Whether we esteem them or not, considering where and how they fit is essential to deciding their fate. This is a job that we cannot shirk, for everything that we do, including nothing, will have a decisive effect.

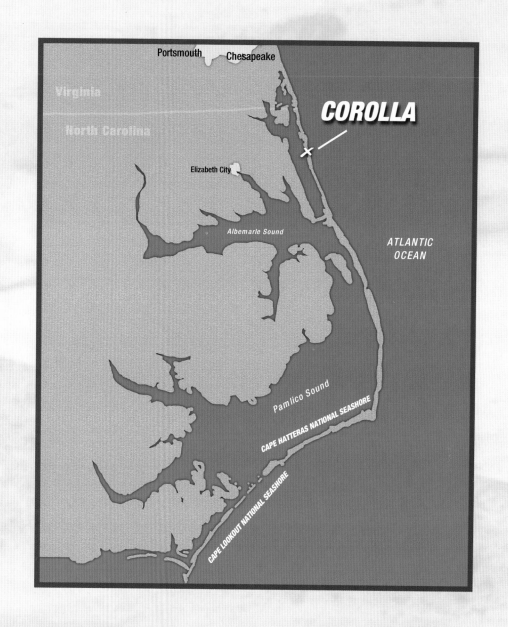

Portsmouth Chesapeake

Virginia

North Carolina

COROLLA

Elizabeth City

Albemarle Sound

ATLANTIC
OCEAN

Pamlico Sound

CAPE HATTERAS NATIONAL SEASHORE

CAPE LOOKOUT NATIONAL SEASHORE

Chapter 2   WHERE THE PAVED ROAD ENDS

The Currituck Banker horses are possibly the oldest surviving American horse breed.

WHERE THE PAVED ROAD ENDS

At one time they numbered in the thousands. They grazed in the marshes and drifted out to the beach in the hot summer months to escape biting insects and catch the sea breeze. Horses have been inhabitants of the North Carolina Outer Banks for centuries, sharing the shifting islands with other free-roaming livestock, including cattle, pigs, goats, and sheep. An article in *National Geographic* stated that between 5,000 and 6,000 horses roamed the Outer Banks in 1926.

For hundreds of years, free-ranging animals far outnumbered humans on this difficult-to-access, difficult-to-homestead barrier island chain. Once or twice a year, locals held branding roundups to establish ownership of new calves and foals. The rest of the time, the animals were unattended.

How did these horses come to live on the North Carolina coast? Legends proclaim them survivors of wrecked Spanish galleons, and, indeed, their bloodlines and physical appearance are Spanish. The most con-

vincing evidence, however, indicates that Banker horses are the descendants of escaped or abandoned domestic stock used by locals. Shipwrecks may have contributed a few horses to the herds, but they are unlikely to be the primary source for the foundation stock.

Although Spain mostly confined its colonizing efforts in the eastern United States to Florida, Georgia, and South Carolina, it sent expeditions farther north. The Eastern Seaboard, however, seemed relatively valueless to Spanish authorities because there were no large deposits of gold, large cities to loot, or concentrated populations to enslave. Throughout the 1500s, European explorers sailed the waters north of Cape Romain, South Carolina, and Chesapeake Bay, searching for places to establish a colony or for a passage linking the Atlantic with the Pacific. These scout ships probably carried few, if any, horses.

Some speculate that Spanish explorers attempted to colonize the coast of North Carolina and left horses behind when the colonies failed. Most historians believe this unlikely. In 1526 Lucas Vasquez de Ayllon established two short-lived settlements, the first of which may have been as far north as the mouth of the Cape Fear River, but this is a long way from the Outer Banks. Spanish Jesuits from Florida established a mission on the lower Chesapeake Bay in 1570, but Indians killed all nine priests the next year. Neither location appears to be a likely source for the Banker horses, nor are there feral herds at Cape Fear or on the western margins of Chesapeake Bay. Most of the feral horses on the East Coast are in places Spaniards are known not to have lived, and it appears that Spain founded no other settlements as far north as the Outer Banks.

BONNIE S. URQUHART

Before the sea-to-sand fence was built, horses routinely strolled into Corolla Village to graze on lush lawns.

It is unlikely Banker horses originated from either early Spanish or English attempts at colonizing North America. Like their Spanish predecessors, the Englishmen who scoured the North Carolina coast in 1584 traveled light and probably did not carry horses. Sir Richard Grenville's expedition did obtain horses in the West Indies in 1585 — animals shown in John White's watercolor of the English camp on Puerto Rico. The 108 men Grenville left on Roanoke Island ran low on provisions. There is no record of them eating horses, but they did eat their watchdogs — presumably the supply of livestock had been exhausted before they turned their appetites to dogs. It is possible that Sir Francis Drake brought horses when he made a pre-arranged visit in June 1586, but after a storm had scattered his fleet, he evacuated the colonists. Any horses left behind may have helped sustain the fifteen men that Grenville dropped off a few weeks later or may have ended up in native cookpots.

It is unclear whether John White's uncoordinated flotillas carried any horses when they sailed for Chesapeake Bay in 1587. When White stopped at Roanoke Island to check on Grenville's men, the pilot refused to take them farther, forcing them to found the settlement on Roanoke Island. After returning to England for supplies, White found the Roanoke colony abandoned in 1590 — no people, livestock, or even much wildlife. Seventeen years passed before England

made another attempt at establishing a presence in North America. Permanent English settlement and large-scale importation of livestock began at Jamestown, founded in what is now Virginia in 1607.

Seventeenth-century settlers came by long, difficult routes across the Atlantic, usually without livestock, and purchased farm animals from the Spanish ranches in the Caribbean. The cattle, hogs, sheep, goats, and horses raised there were of top quality, bred to be hardy and durable, and were much more likely to survive the shorter voyage to the colonies. Buying from Spanish ranches also eliminated the unpleasantness of feeding, watering, and cleaning up after animals on a protracted transatlantic voyage. In many cases, settlers could not afford to import animals from England, and buying from the Spanish ranchers was an economic necessity.

When the English Parliament imposed a tax on fences in 1670, subsistence farmers moved most of their livestock to islands and peninsulas, effectively penning them with water. A peninsula required only a fence at some narrow spot to contain the livestock, and a barrier island required no fence at all. Most of the land grazed by livestock, especially on the barrier chains, was considered unsuitable for any other use. Islands and necks all along the East Coast, including Boston Neck, Staten Island, Point Judith, Rhode Island, and many parts of Long Island, supported free-range livestock. Roundups were held once or twice a year to divide and brand stock and remove certain animals to the mainland. Breeding stock remained to roam freely and multiply at will.

Some of the farmers and stockmen who had settled on the necks along the northern margin of Albemarle Sound may have turned livestock loose on the Banks before the Carolina Charter, a land grant bequeathed by England's Charles II in 1663 to eight aristocratic supporters.

The first officially sanctioned settlement on the Outer Banks was established in 1663 on Colington Island, near Nags Head. Its chief sources of income were whale oil and livestock. Records are patchy, but in all likelihood free-roaming domestic stock was well established on the Outer Banks by the early 1700s. The largest herds probably ranged along Currituck Sound and on Core Banks. Gary Dunbar wrote in his *Historical Geography of the North Carolina Outer Banks* that by 1776 the Banks were covered with cattle, sheep, and hogs, and "the few inhabitants living on the banks (were) chiefly persons whose estates consist in livestock."

The earliest cattle and horses freed to these islands were probably purely Spanish in ancestry, for the earliest colonial farm animals were Spanish stock bought (or, according to some accounts, stolen) in the West Indies. Author and veterinarian D. Phillip Sponenberg writes that around 1700, the purely Spanish horse could be found from the Carolinas to Florida, west through Tennessee, and throughout all of the western mountains and Great Plains. As time went on, fine horses were imported from England and elsewhere, and America herself began to develop unique breeds.

The Narragansett Pacer, developed in New England, quickly became popular throughout Colonial America. Its heritage included a strong Spanish component, perhaps influenced by the blood of English and Dutch horses imported in the early 1600s. Initially, mainland roads were poor, little more than paths through the forest. The Narragansett Pacer was a sure-footed horse with an uncommonly smooth gait and great endurance, making it possible to travel the many miles between communities comfortably. During the 1700s, colonists prized these horses and bred large numbers of them. Paul Revere was reportedly astride one on his famous ride.

As roads improved, the Americans came to prefer horse-drawn conveyances to riding astride and favored trotters as carriage animals. Many considered it sacrilegious to race horses at a gallop under saddle, but it was morally acceptable to race at the trot because the horses weren't traveling at top speed. Harness breeds gained steadily in popularity. Breeders lost interest in the Narragansett Pacer, and the breed became extinct in the late 1800s.

Quarter Horses originated in the Carolinas and Virginia. As with the origins of most breeds, there is argument about details. One of the foundation sires was

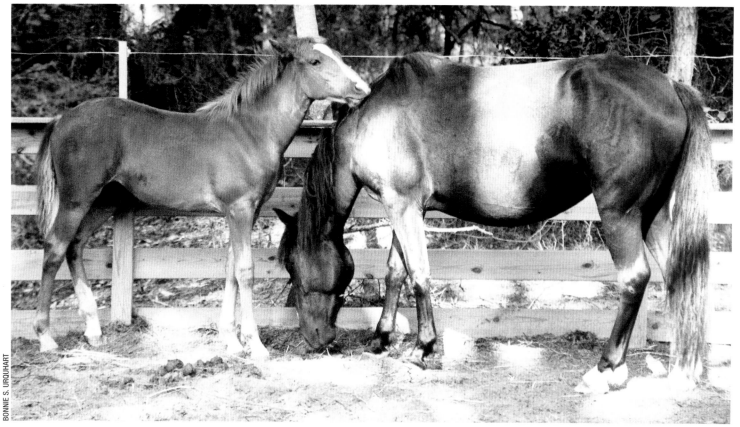

BONNIE S. URQUHART

Visitors to the Currituck Lighthouse can get close to horses penned on the grounds.

Janus, a spotted English Thoroughbred imported to Virginia in 1746. The Thoroughbred was new then and Arabian blood dominated. Janus was a grandson of a founding sire, the Godolphin Arabian. Consequently, Janus was not built like today's Thoroughbred, or even a modern Quarter Horse, but was a compact, muscular 14.1 hands tall. In the twenty-four years he stood at stud in North Carolina and southern Virginia, he successfully infused the Spanish-based local stock with his genes. Many of his offspring displayed his speed, endurance, and spotted coat.

These breeding trends probably influenced the genes

BONNIE S. URQUHART

The author's sons, Mark Bryan and Keith, visit the horses penned at the Corolla lighthouse.

of the Banker horses. *The Story of Ocracoke Island*, compiled by Hyde County in 1976, makes mention of the Pea Island horses being larger than the usual Banker pony because they "came from the original quarter-bred horse."

Just how Spanish is the North Carolina Banker horse of today? Dr. E. Gus Cothran, a researcher at the University of Kentucky, has studied the relationship of Banker horses to other breeds. In a project funded by the Eastern National Park and Monument Association, Cothran drew blood samples from North American coastal horses and studied seventeen genetic marker systems in an effort to determine lineage and understand genetic variation within the herds. His work provides a scientific basis for discussing the origins of these horses.

Cothran revealed that the horses of the North Carolina coast — Corolla, Shackleford and Carrot Islands, and Ocracoke — have more genetically in common with one another than with other breeds. In his paper "The Banker Horse Genetic Research Program," Cothran explains his belief that "the feral horses on Cape Hatteras descended from a single population, although other introductions may have taken place later." Their genes show Spanish ancestry, but do not clarify just what that ancestry was. He says the Corolla horses are a unique population with low genetic variability and show no close resemblance to any particular horse breed. Cothran believes that horses obtained by colonists in the Caribbean were ancestors to both the Banker horses and the saddle and harness breeds, and he believes it quite possible that both lines descend from the Narragansett Pacer.

Some articles tell us that the Conquistadors were riding Spanish Mustangs when they first set hoof on this continent, but this is not strictly true. Mustang is the term applied to the horses after they had escaped to the wild. The Spanish did not bring wild or feral horses to America; they brought fine, purebred Jennets, Barbs,

and probably a few Arabians, mostly to the breeding ranches in the Caribbean. East Coast Jennet-based Spanish feral herds can arguably be termed Mustangs in their present state, but Jennets were not Mustangs upon arrival in the New World. And though the modern Spanish Mustang is a breed based on original Jennet bloodlines, the breed registry was established during the twentieth century, not the sixteenth.

Are any Banker horses registered Spanish Mustangs? Robert Brislawn of Oshoto, Wyoming, who sought to preserve the original Spanish-blooded Mustang by finding and breeding the few remaining horses believed to be of authentic Spanish blood, founded the Spanish Mustang Registry in 1957. In the 1970s certain members of the Ocracoke herd were admitted into this registry, but since then no other horses from East Coast feral populations have been included. Many present-day Ocracoke horses descend from an Andalusian stallion outcrossed into the herd in the 1970s. Andalusians are not Spanish Mustangs. They are two different breeds, and, therefore, the Ocracoke horses descending from these matings are regarded as crossbreeds; as such, the Mustang Registry considers these animals ineligible for registration.

Some wild horse enthusiasts look to the number of lumbar vertebrae as an indicator of authentic Spanish bloodlines. Spanish horses tend to have one less vertebra than the usual six. But according to Cothran, counting vertebrae proves little. As a species, all horses have either five or six lumbar vertebrae or show a partial fusion of the fifth and sixth. While many or most Spanish horses have five lumbar vertebrae, so do many other breeds. This trait is very common in Arabians and regularly occurs in other breeds as well, even Thoroughbreds.

So what exactly are Banker horses? We know they have descended from Spanish stock, maybe by way of the Narragansett Pacer. It is probable that outside influ- ences have introduced new genes episodically, but for the most part these animals have been bred Banker-to- Banker, resulting in a Spanish-blooded horse with unique characteristics. As such, they could be the oldest surviving American horse breed.

The Currituck Banker horses are genetically most similar to the Ocracoke herd, but are closely related to the horses living on islands as far south as Shackleford and, to a lesser degree, to the horses of Cumberland Island, Georgia. This genetic uniformity of Banker

Rolling in the sand kills insects and lets the horse scratch itchy spots.

BONNIE S. URQUHART

horses further discredits the shipwreck legends. The horses of Cumberland Island, in an area where Spaniards certainly did settle, are very similar to the horses of the Outer Banks, where Spaniards certainly did not settle. Moreover, Cothran's observation that the Banks and Cumberland herds have more in common with New World Spanish horses than with Jennets indicates that the progenitors of both herds must have arrived after those breeds appeared. In the case of the Bankers, this was probably at no time in the sixteenth century. It appears that most or all of the Cumberland horses descend from stock brought there by the Carnegie family in the late 1800s.

The uniformity of the Banker herds is also influenced by the dynamic nature of barrier islands. A powerful storm can literally cut an island in half, creating an inlet where there was solid ground the day before. Conversely, sediment can fill in old inlets to create solid ground. These banks continually merge and separate. During severe weather, dramatic changes in features can take place over days or even hours.

In the stretch between Portsmouth Island and the Virginia line alone, more than two dozen inlets have existed since Colonial times. At this writing, three remain open. The island livestock migrated to whatever solid ground existed, becoming stranded from the rest when an inlet blocked old routes. Following pony pennings, horses were often sold from island to island, remixing the herds.

The barrier-island environment was challenging for livestock and humans alike. Herds and homesteads were equally vulnerable to the wrath of storms. In the early days, communities were usually established on the more protected mainland, leaving the banks largely to livestock.

In more recent times, many of North Carolina's beautiful barrier islands became popular with vacationers, swelling the seasonal population tremendously in communities such as Nags Head, Kill Devil Hills, and Kitty Hawk. While growing hordes of tourists flocked to the Outer Banks for the summer, developers and boosters worked to attract more visitors by building a bridge and causeway from Roanoke Island to Nags Head and a bridge across Currituck Sound. In 1932 the state of North Carolina took over the bridges and paved a highway connecting them. In 1933 two hurricanes inflicted great damage on the Banks, leveling dunes and dwellings. These and lesser storms regularly buried the blacktop.

Further development depended on the highway, which depended on successful beach stabilization, which depended on establishing an artificial dune line held in place by vegetation. Between 1933 and 1940 the Civilian Conservation Corps installed hundreds of miles of sand fencing to catch the sand and build the dune line, then anchored it with the living mesh of roots from carefully planted grass.

This vegetation looked like lunch to the roaming live-stock, and they cropped the sprouts as quickly as they appeared. In 1935 the North Carolina General Assembly passed legislation requiring livestock owners north of Hatteras Inlet to fence in their animals. The days of free-roaming herds had officially ended.

Most of the ranchers did not own large tracts of land and had allowed their animals to graze in marshland owned by local hunt clubs or absentees. They did not have the resources to maintain stock profitably on their own property. Suddenly, families comprising genera-tions of herdsmen were forced to find another liveli-hood. Within a few years, the number of substantial livestock operations on the Outer Banks was reduced from about fifty to seven or eight.

Some horses evaded capture and retreated to the most remote reaches of the Banks. They did not spend much time visiting human beings, but when they did wander into a village, they peacefully coexisted with the residents, who, for the most part, enjoyed having them around.

The village of Corolla, pronounced kuh-RAH-la, sprang up around the Currituck Beach Lighthouse (1872) and Life Saving Station (1874) and acquired its present name when the post office opened around the turn of the century. Corolla was effectively cut off from the rest of the world and didn't get electricity until 1955. Until 1973 the only land access was by a long, rutty, unpaved state road from the south. Alternatively, one could take the beach, driving between the high and low tidemarks, but this was often an unreliable and risky means of travel.

Developers paved a road north to the village but restricted access until 1984. When the state took over the road, the outside world descended. Beautiful Corolla was secluded no longer. Before 1986 there were only thirty-five full-time residents. A decade later that number had more than tripled, but the bulk of the pop-ulation influx came from thousands of people eager to rent seasonal beach homes or just visit for the day.

Magazines and billboards touted Corolla as an "undiscovered paradise," and people came flocking to the "empty beaches." Cars zoomed around the bends of N.C. Highway 12. Condos sprang up like the lesions of a fast-breeding virus. Prices were high, but there was no shortage of wealthy vacationers. The juxtaposition of sleek wild horses and expensive condominiums, nature and progress inspired powerful opinions on both sides.

The dark horses that often crossed the road at night knew nothing about the impatient drivers that flew down the new roadways. In 1989, after six horses were killed in one accident, Corolla residents and visitors united to create the Corolla Wild Horse Fund. Their mission was to guard the Corolla horses against the human invasion and to preserve their wildness.

The horses needed government protection, but as non-

BONNIE S. URQUHART

Humans must stay fifty yards from the horses.

native wildlife they were ineligible for any. Hunt clubs complained that the wild horses ate the food planted for the waterfowl and asked the North Carolina Wildlife Resources Commission to remove the herd — but the horses were not native wildlife and therefore not its concern. Currituck County looked to the state for help. The state bounced the responsibility back to the county.

As Corolla residents wrestled with red tape, horses died. The Corolla Wild Horse Fund outfitted horses with reflective collars to make them more visible to motorists, sprayed them with glow-in-the-dark paint, and posted signs along Highway 12 warning motorists to slow down because of "Horses On Road at Any Time." These tactics helped to reduce, but not eliminate, fatalities. Some signs were even stolen by vacationers in search of souvenirs.

The fatalities were devastating. In 1990 a mare known as Bay Girl delivered a foal that was to be named Freedom. This birth was eagerly anticipated, for the mare's previous foal had been killed by a car. The day following his birth, the newborn was found floating in a pond, umbilical cord still attached. His wounds told the story — someone had hit him with a car and then thrown his little body into the water.

Eventually, the horses were termed a "cultural resource" worthy of protection. The Corolla Wild Horse Fund finally convinced the county to establish a wild horse sanctuary where trapping, taking, tormenting, injuring, or killing the horses was prohibited. But problems continued.

In a small population like the one on Currituck Banks, it is important to maintain genetic variety in order to avoid inbreeding. Sometimes this necessity is at odds with practicality. At one point, a large percentage of foals born happened to be male, and as they grew older, they presented a unique problem.

Usually colts are driven from the herd when they reach puberty. They form bachelor bands and keep one another company until about age five or six, when they are mature enough to start their own bands. The Currituck colts had no incentive to head north to eat marsh grass. Lured by the lush lawns of Corolla, they stayed, chasing mares around in adolescent ardor and exhausting the mature stallions.

These colts ranged mostly in populated areas, and once they matured, there was sure to be fighting over the few available mares. Tourists would surely get caught in it. In 1990 the Corolla Wild Horse Fund proposed to geld bachelor colts, reducing friction and creating a more stable herd.

This approach was controversial. If something unfortunate happened to the herd stallions, the colts would be the only hope for the continuity of bloodlines. With so many fatalities, this was certainly a concern. Opponents of the plan reasoned that wild horses should live without human intervention, beneficial or detrimental, and that a gelding is not a truly wild horse. The proposal to geld was defeated.

Aggressive attempts at public education did not afford the horses adequate protection. While most visitors respected the ordinances, some were incredibly reckless. Vacationers that might be a little nervous mounting a well-trained rental horse for an amble down the beach actually felt safe in putting their children upon the backs of these unbroken, unpredictable horses for a photograph! One tourist lured a curious two-year-old colt up onto the deck of a beach house with food. The animal fell and was seriously injured.

County ordinance required people to stay fifty yards from the horses. Too many tourists couldn't resist the impulse to feed and pet them when they thought nobody was watching. Reports of kicks and bites were common.

People also didn't stop to consider that a horse's digestive system is adapted to eating grass. The animals might like the taste of pickles or peanut butter and jelly, but human food can make them very sick. Many tourists fed the horses whatever was handy. Some even left plastic bags of apples and carrots as treats. The animals didn't understand that the bag was not part of the meal and consumed the entire offering, unaware that intestinal blockage was likely afterward.

Domestic horses are prone to colic, but Banker horses rarely develop digestive problems on their diet of grasses. When the horses were left to themselves, the rare instances of colic were usually due to sand ingestion. Once tourists appeared on the scene, colic became frequent and potentially life threatening.

Many well-meaning people were ignorant of normal horse behavior. They thought that a pair of thousand-pound stallions intent on serious struggle were "playing" and approached closely in hopes of petting one. They thought that new foals were cute and chased them around behind their protective mothers. Horses are at their moodiest during the breeding season, which coincides with tourist season.

A normal horse, acting as its instincts have commanded over millions of years of evolution, was justified in biting, kicking, or flattening the intruders. But animals that injure people are often destroyed or confined, whether or not the action was appropriate from the animal's perspective. Animals accustomed to the presence of humans may appear docile but remain unpredictable wild animals that can revert to dangerous instinctive behavior when stressed.

Corolla Wild Horse Fund volunteers donated incalculable amounts of time to locating the herd and keeping tourists at a distance. But these volunteers had jobs and families vying for their time, and there were too few of them to avert all potential tragedies.

The fund built a fence with collected money and donated land, material, and labor, hoping to encourage the horses to stay within the uninhabited, protected two

thousand acres of the Currituck Natural Wildlife Refuge. The horses simply walked around the fence to resume grazing on the greenness of Corolla.

In 1995 an improved sea-to-sound barrier was completed, this one reaching well out into the water to keep the horses north of town. It took two days to herd the horses north of the fence, where they joined other bands that ranged as far north as Back Bay National Wildlife Refuge. The horses immediately began to test the fence for weak spots. One pushed through where a cable was loose and was herded back.

Some observers scoffed at the fence, asserting that it wouldn't deter horses known for their swimming ability. The average depth of Currituck Sound is only five feet, and few areas exceed ten feet. Any enterprising horse, they argued, would easily find a way around.

Butterscotch, an ingenious lead mare, proved them right by persistently leading her herd back to the lush vegetation of the golf courses and green sod lawns. In one remarkable incident, she traveled north until she found a sand bar that extended out into the sound and reached 1,500 feet beyond the end of the fence. She and her friends sloshed through foot-deep water and re-entered Corolla well south of the barrier.

This adventure resulted in the death of Grecko, her black yearling son, in June 1995. Grecko wandered into the road near a supermarket around two a.m. and was thrown ninety-one feet by an eighteen-year-old driver,

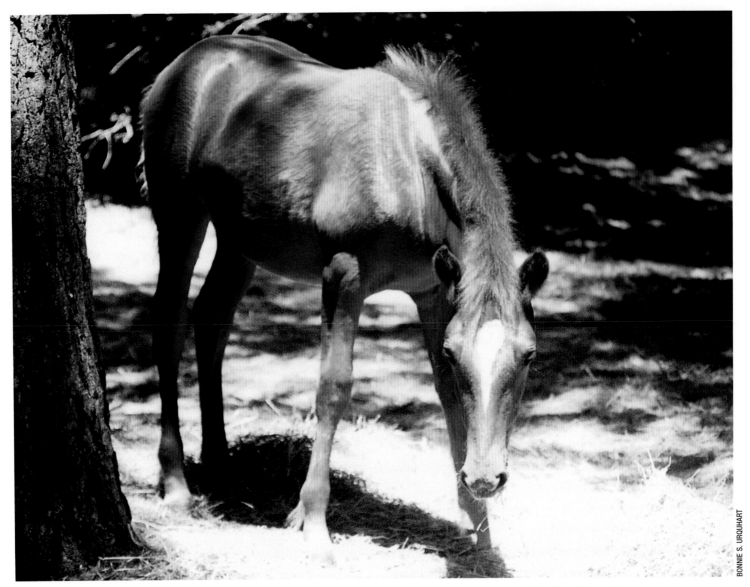

The Corolla Wild Horse Fund has taken various steps to protect the feral herds.

who was later charged with possession of alcohol.

By the fall of 1995, sixteen horses had been killed, and others had been injured. Within the year, the Corolla Wild Horse Fund agreed that the only way to protect the horses that persistently breached the barrier was to relocate them on the mainland, in a protected area near Smithfield, North Carolina.

The rest of the horses seemed content to stay to the north of the barrier, living as wild on the undeveloped land. Then, in 1999, reports of wild horses raiding yards, trash cans, and a produce stand made the news as a stallion named Little Red Man and his herd repeatedly came around the barrier to forage in Corolla. He was relocated with his mares to a four-hundred-acre hunt club overlooking Currituck Sound. That same year, a black mare was killed on a Corolla road, orphaning her foal. And because there is no barrier on the north end of their prescribed range, sometimes horses cross the Virginia line and visit populated areas there.

The development boom continues on Currituck Banks, and a proposed bridge connecting Corolla directly to the mainland would encourage more visitors. Although the northern reaches of Currituck Banks remain roadless, growth there has been explosive. But recently, Currituck County officials assembled members of the Corolla Wild Horse Fund, the Currituck National Wildlife Refuge, and the North Carolina National Estuarine Research Reserve to work out a management plan. As a result, federal and state agencies have incorporated the Currituck horses into their missions. Management practices now include maintaining a herd of fewer than sixty individuals; blocking wild-horse access to the developed areas of Corolla and Virginia and relocating horses that frequent populated areas; monitoring health status; maintaining enclosures for a few horses at the Whalehead Club or the Currituck Beach Lighthouse; and using private pastures within the off-road area.

These horses and their ancestors, possibly the oldest surviving American horse breed, have ranged freely over the dunes of Currituck County for hundreds of years. Today, they owe their liberty and protection to the efforts of advocates who battled relentlessly on their behalf. Thanks to the work of the Corolla Wild Horse Fund and support from concerned individuals and groups, this unique aspect of Corolla's cultural and historical heritage has been preserved.

The Corolla horses are co-existing with humanity, but there are undeveloped lots of prime beach front to the north. If developers improve access with the proposed bridge, the horses could face a problem similar to what they encountered in Corolla Village. If the wildlife refuge officials determine that the horses are competing with the wildlife for available food, they can deny them the privilege of grazing the refuge. Today there is balance. Tomorrow there may not be.

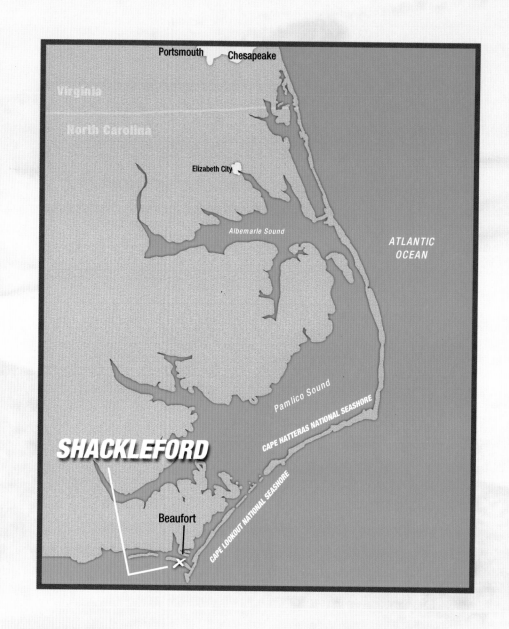

Portsmouth Chesapeake

Virginia

North Carolina

Elizabeth City

Albemarle Sound

ATLANTIC
OCEAN

Pamlico Sound

CAPE HATTERAS NATIONAL SEASHORE

SHACKLEFORD

CAPE LOOKOUT NATIONAL SEASHORE

Beaufort

Chapter 3   THE SHIFTING SANDS OF SHACKLEFORD

Silhouettes on the dunes, two Shackleford fillies graze at sunset.

THE SHIFTING SANDS
OF SHACKLEFORD

Feral horses have lived on the islands of the Cape Lookout National Seashore for centuries, just as they roamed Ocracoke and Currituck islands to the north. Now they remain only on Shackleford Banks, a narrow ribbon of sand roughly eleven miles long, lying perpendicular to the southernmost end of Core Banks in North Carolina. There are, of course, the familiar shipwreck legends to explain the arrival of the horses. The shoals off Cape Lookout and along the banks are certainly treacherous, and ships often carried horses and other livestock.

Even equine biologist Jay Kirkpatrick, in his book *Into the Wind, Wild Horses of North America*, suggests shipwrecks might have brought horses to Shackleford as early as 1565. A 1991 study by Robin Goodloe of the U.S. Fish & Wildlife Service's Georgia Ecological Service's field office revealed that the Shackleford horses are genetically similar to the horses of Ocracoke Island (which genetically resemble Standardbreds), as well as several draft breeds.

But because human settlements were successful on the Shackleford and Core banks for many decades, it is more probable that most, if not all, of these horses descended from the livestock turned loose by mainlanders or left behind when the owners resettled on the mainland. Few records exist, and the horses have been around for so long that many generations of residents grew up believing that the horses had always been there. Through the 1800s locals frequently informed island visitors that the horses were a native species.

The first known residents were the Coree Indians, who had lived on and around the islands since prehistoric times. In fact, the name *Core Banks* may be a diminutive of *Coree*. John Shackleford purchased Shackleford Banks in 1714, giving it its current name. English colonists inhabited the island in the 1760s, and by the mid-1800s, Shackleford Banks was home to more than six hundred residents in several communities.

Diamond City was the largest town, situated on the

east end of Shackleford near the Cape Lookout Lighthouse, before Bardens Inlet divided Core Banks from Shackleford. Some believe the city took its name from the distinctive diamond pattern of the lighthouse. The island supported an oyster house, a factory that extracted oil from porpoises, a crab-packing plant, schoolhouses, businesses, and churches. The residents' sheep, goats, cattle, and horses freely roamed the island, often wandering north to Core Banks. After a particularly damaging storm in 1899, the San Ciriaco Hurricane, most of the residents moved to the more stable ground of the mainland, many settling in the Promised Land section of Morehead City or on Harkers Island. Today two telephone poles and a few old cemeteries are the only visible evidence that this area used to be settled.

Shackleford is generally higher than Core Banks and has a more varied landscape, including thirty-five-foot dunes at the western end. Vegetation was dense before early settlers cleared much of the maritime forest, and in this challenging climate trees did not grow back easily. The free-roaming livestock multiplied and overgrazed the island. Foraging sheep mowed grasses to the ground and damaged root systems. Goats destroyed trees and shrubs. Severe hurricanes in the 1800s destroyed most of the remaining woods. Today bushes and shrubs outnumber trees on the island.

Because Bardens Inlet did not separate Shackleford from Core Banks until the Hurricane of 1933, horses and other animals were free to wander the length of the islands. Edmund Ruffin, an agricultural authority from Virginia, visited the area about 1858. He noted in his 1861 book, *Agricultural, Geological, and Descriptive Sketches of Lower North Carolina and the Similar Adjacent Lands*, that the horses were

all of small size, with rough and shaggy coats, and long manes. They are generally ugly. Their hoofs, in many cases, grow to unusual lengths. They are capable of great endurance of labor and hardship, and live so roughly, that others from abroad seldom live a year on such food and under such exposure.

The 'horse-pennings' are much attended, and are very interesting festivals for all the residents of the neighboring main-land. There are few adults, residing within a day's sailing of the horse-pen, that have not attended one or more of these exciting scenes. A strong enclosure, called the horse-pen, is made at a narrow part of the reef, and suitable in other respects for the purpose—with a connected strong fence, stretching quite across the reef. All of the many proprietors of the horses, and with many assistants, drive (in deer-hunters' phrase) from the remote extremities of the reef, and easily bring, and then encircle, all the horses to the fence and near to the pen.

A Shackleford Banks stallion keeps watch.

There the drivers are reinforced by hundreds of volunteers from among the visitors and amateurs, and the circle is narrowed until all the horses are forced into the pen, where any of them may be caught and confined. Then the young colts, distinguished by being with their mothers, are marked by their owner's brand. All of the many persons who came to buy horses, and the proprietors who wish to capture and remove any for use, or subsequent sale, then make their selections. After the price is fixed, each selected animal is caught and haltered, and immediately subjected to a rider. This is not generally very difficult—or the difficulties and the consequent accidents and mishaps to the riders are only sufficient to increase the interest and fun of the scene, and the pleasure and triumph of the actors. After the captured horse has been thrown, and sufficiently choked by the halter, he is suffered to rise, mounted by some bold and experienced rider and breaker, and forced into a neighboring creek, with a bottom of mud, stiff and deep enough to fatigue the horse, and to render him incapable of making more use of his feet than to struggle to avoid sinking too deep into the mire. Under these circumstances, he soon yields to his rider—and rarely afterwards does one resist.

Mainland residents in Atlantic and surrounding communities often visited Core Banks to slaughter hogs and cattle when they needed meat. Jean Day writes in her book *Banker Ponies* that some residents spent the summer in cottages on Core Banks.

The Cape Lookout National Seashore was established in March 1966, extending about fifty-five miles from Ocracoke Inlet to the north, to Beaufort Inlet in the south. Cape Lookout seems destined to escape the commercialism and population growth of the Cape Hatteras area. It can only be reached by private boat or ferry, and there are no roads and few facilities. Situated on the flyway, it is frequented by at least 275 species of birds, both residents and seasonal visitors, including the bald eagle, peregrine falcon, and piping plover. The island also supports loggerhead turtles, rabbits, raccoons, snakes, river otters, and many other varieties of wildlife.

The bands of feral horses vary widely in size, six to sixteen being typical. A herd stallion generally will not permit another male to remain past puberty but occasionally makes exceptions. A young subordinate stud is sometimes tolerated as long as he remembers his place and does not attempt to mate with the mares. Two-male harems were uncommon on Shackleford in the early 1980s, when the sex ratio was typically two females to every male. During the late 1990s, the ratio was closer to one to one. Perhaps this explains the increase in two-stallion herds.

Ordinarily, wild horses don't defend a territory. Instead they maintain a "sphere of intolerance." The stallion grazes his band of mares within a preferred range, attacking any rival males that violate his invisible boundaries. Shackleford Banks, however, has the distinction of being one of the only places in the world where biologists observed horses defending territories rather than simply guarding harems. This territoriality is due in part to the narrowness of the island and the low dunes and grasslands that allow the defending stallion to detect intruders from a distance. (A single Assateague stallion, Comma, was observed displaying similar territorial behaviors on a similarly narrow, treeless stretch of island.)

On Shackleford, territorial stallions controlled the sections with the lushest grass, outcompeting weaker rivals. Mares associated with dominant males grazed an average of two extra hours per day and displayed increased fertility. Dr. Daniel Rubenstein, who studied these horses in the 1970s and '80s, was surprised to find these territorial stallions maintaining very large harems of mares. While his studies were in progress, around 1980, an increase of bachelor males upset the social order by overthrowing the older harem studs. These younger stallions divided up the mares, and the territorial system dissolved. His project, "Behavioral Ecology of Island Feral Horses," was published in a 1981 issue of *Equine Veterinary Journal*.

BONNIE S. URQUHART

The Cape Lookout Lighthouse is across the inlet from Shackleford Banks.

The Shackleford Banks horses make their own watering holes by digging in the sand with their hooves until they reach the water table. A lens of fairly fresh water floats atop the heavier saline layer, and the sand serves to filter out some of the salt. Sometimes they dig so deeply that only their rumps are visible as they imbibe from the pool. The fresh water can be slow to seep into the depression, and pony herds often spend hours near the watering spot to ensure that each herd member gets enough. Spring rains create seasonal fresh

Overgrazing and overproduction take their toll.

water pools — hoofprints along the edges advertise that the horses use this source as well.

CEDAR ISLAND

Historically, horses grazed other islands in the area, including Hog Island, Browns Island, Harbor Island, Chain Shot Island, and Cedar Island.

Steve Yeomans, a young Cedar Island horseman, remembers when many of the locals would turn surplus horses out to join the herds in the marsh. Round-ups were held in the summer. About thirty people would spread out to form a chain and "walk them in." Once captured, the horses were branded, received veterinary care, and had their hooves trimmed if necessary. Most were freed back to the marshes.

The Cedar Island horses were small, 13 hands at best, and carried a mixture of pony and Spanish bloodlines. They only lived ten or fifteen years. "I never saw an old Banker, except for one that was turned out late in his life," commented Yeomans.

A few still remained on Cedar until June 1997, when the free-roaming population was rounded up and tested for equine infectious anemia, a potentially lethal fly-borne disease. All of the domestic horses at a local riding stable had tested positive for the virus, and authorities were unable to trace the source of the infection. As it turned out, the local free-roaming horses were the disease reservoir. Of the fifteen horses tested, thirteen

BONNIE S. URQUHART

When fresh water is scarce, the horses dig down to the water table and create their own watering holes.

were positive for the virus and were euthanized, marking the end of Cedar Island's feral herds.

Equine infectious anemia (or swamp fever) is a viral disease caused by a retrovirus similar to the one that causes AIDS in humans. After an incubation period of two to four weeks, infected horses may show symptoms such as fever, weakness, weight loss, lack of coordination, and swelling of the legs and underbelly. Horses that survive an acute attack or contract a less severe case often develop a mild, chronic form with occasional exacerbations, or become asymptomatic carriers that can potentially infect the rest of the herd. The USDA states that one-fifth of a teaspoon of blood from an infected horse during a feverish episode carries enough live virus to infect 10,000 horses.

Robert Oglesby, DVM, writes in the online *Horseman's Advisor* that mosquitoes do not spread the disease because of the low numbers of virus particles they transmit and the small amounts of blood they move from horse to horse. Horse flies feed by slashing open the skin and lapping the blood, thereby moving more blood from victim to victim. North Carolina state law requires that all horses with positive Coggins tests, the test for equine infectious anemia, must be quarantined or destroyed to prevent them from infecting others. Because the disease can only be spread by fresh blood, and blood dries rapidly on the mouthparts of biting flies, horses are considered quarantined if they are

BONNIE S. URQUHART

Shackleford horses are tolerant of people...

rific swimmers, and could even cross wide, swift currents in the channel separating Harkers Island from the mainland with a child astride. He told of a mare that would not flinch when a large gun was shot from between her ears.

Steve Yeomans' grandmother lived on Shackleford Banks when people still occupied its sandy expanse and livestock roamed freely. Shackleford did not become a part of the national seashore until 1986. At that time, people no longer resided on the island year-round. But many mainland residents who owned land on Shackleford maintained fishing cabins and other shelters for seasonal use and still held pony, sheep, and cattle pennings on the Fourth of July every year. Upon acquiring the island, the Park Service razed the buildings and allowed natural processes to resume.

Around this time, the livestock census was 108 horses, 89 cattle, 144 sheep, and 121 goats. The Park Service removed sheep, cattle, and goats from the island, grudgingly permitting the horses to remain as an exotic species because the public wanted them

stabled two hundred yards from other horses.

Banker ponies on Cedar Island and elsewhere had long been valued for riding and drafting throughout the area. "Not all of them make good riding horses," Yeomans explained. "Some are unrideable. They're just too smart. Most of them are easier to train than other breeds. Once you get them used to a saddle and bridle, they'll do anything in the world for you." Some were ter-

BONNIE S. URQUHART

...but swiftly shepherd their youngsters away from intruders.

there. They multiplied rapidly, from 108 individuals in 1982 to a 1996 high of over 240.

A management crisis developed. The equine population overgrazed the island and strained the ecosystem. Nature's way of keeping the balance is to allow surplus animals to die of starvation when food sources are depleted. If the Park Service did not intervene, large numbers of horses would succumb to preventable deaths, and in the process certain native plants could also be grazed out of existence.

CARROT ISLAND

This had already recently happened on Carrot Island, a small, sandy island lying to the west of Shackleford. Carrot, along with Town Marsh, Bird Shoal, and Horse Island, is part of the Rachel Carson component of the North Carolina National Estuarine Research Reserve, named in honor of the noted environmentalist and author. Carrot Island appears on maps as early as 1777 and was the site of a fishery in the early 1800s. In the 1920s the U.S. Army Corps of engineers dredged Taylors Creek and deposited the sand on Carrot, building it higher and increasing its stability.

Feral horses have lived on Carrot since the late 1940s (which, incidentally, was around the time Rachel Carson did her research in that area). Apparently, a local doctor named Luther

BONNIE S. URQUHART

Carrot Island, across from the busy Beaufort waterfront, remains undeveloped.

Insects and shedding baby fur make this youngster chronically itchy.

Fuller, who also owned horses on Shackleford banks, ran six of his horses on Carrot Island. After Fuller died, the horses lived as wild, sustaining themselves with no human assistance. Their descendants live with minimal human interference today across the creek from the Beaufort waterfront.

In July 1976, about forty acres of the island were almost auctioned off for development. Beaufort residents who enjoyed the wild beauty of the island and its horses took action. After a legal battle, the Nature Conservancy, aided by funds raised by concerned local residents, paid $250,000 for Carrot Island and Bird Shoal. It was agreed that the island would remain forever safe from development. In April 1984, the 2,025-acre Rachel Carson Estuarine Sanctuary was established.

With nothing to curb their fertility, the original horses proliferated and overgrazed the marsh grasses, unbalancing the estuarine ecology. Feral horses also interfered with nesting birds, some of them rare. By 1986 the horse population on this small island had reached sixty-eight. There simply was not enough food for all of them. Mark Hay, an assistant professor of marine fisheries, commented in the *Carteret News Times* that the Carrot Island horses were making what could be a great vegetative system into little more than a sandbox with stubble here and there.

Mother Nature handled the overpopulation problem in her own way during the winter of 1986-87. Famine and parasites killed twenty-nine individuals within a few short months. Once concerned locals realized what was happening, they brought in hay as supplementary feed; but the starving horses, accustomed to native grasses, often refused to eat it.

Spring brought numerous foals, and by August 1988, the herd numbered fifty-one. The North Carolina Division of Marine Fisheries had helped them through the winter of 1987-88 by providing twenty bales of hay each week. A point-well ensured fresh water. But clearly this human assistance could not continue. If the horses were to remain as exotic wildlife, their numbers must be in balance with their environment. Biologists determined that Carrot Island could comfortably sustain between fifteen and twenty-five horses, and in 1988 the state removed thirty-three of fifty-two horses. Nine of the thirty-three removed tested positive for equine infectious anemia and were euthanized. Private individuals adopted the remainder. In 1996 the population was up to thirty, and a dart-gun birth-control program was initiated.

By the late 1990s it became clear that Shackleford would face a similar crisis if the Park Service did not control the equine population. To better understand the relationship of the horses to the native wildlife and vegetation, the Park Service used the research of Gene Wood of Clemson University and Daniel Rubenstein of Princeton University. Data in hand, the National Park Service pondered how best to handle the equine population dilemma.

The National Park Service exists not only to protect natural ecosystems, but also to interpret and educate. Even if the horses can be considered biological nuisances, they are also cultural resources, and the Park Service can neither deport them nor keep them without ignoring part of its mission.

The Shackleford horses are exotics that compete with and disrupt native species and arguably do not belong

there. But the ring-necked pheasant, also an exotic, is permitted to remain on Core Banks, as are feral hogs on Cumberland Island and Sika deer on Assateague. Although horses are entitled to protection under the 1980 General Management Plan, Park Service policy is to intervene when exotic animals or plants "threaten to alter park resources or public health."

One strategy was to remove all of the horses once and for all. The public was generally opposed to this; they liked the horses and wanted them to remain. Many locals

The author encountered this sick Shackleford Banks foal.

grew up on the backs of Banker horses and considered them an important part of their cultural heritage.

The Park Service also considered taking a number of horses off the island and "managing" the rest. Park officials felt that a herd of roughly sixty horses could be self-sustaining. Fewer horses would leave less genetic variability, necessitating an infusion of outside genes periodically to revitalize the gene pool. A roundup could be held and the excess horses adopted by the public. Stallions could be castrated. Mares could be maintained on contraceptives. Although this approach is similar to the management of the Ocracoke Island herd, the National Park Service was not enthusiastic about maintaining a "horse farm" on Shackleford Island. If the horses are to be considered wildlife, officials asserted, then they should be treated as wildlife and left to live as wild animals.

Many locals favored controlling the population though annual roundups, in keeping with local tradition. Horse pennings had been commonplace on these islands for centuries, and it seemed fitting to hold with historical tradition. As on Chincoteague to the north, an annual roundup could stimulate tourism, and proceeds from the sales of young stock could support horse management on the island. The National Park Service opposed this plan, asserting that the potential for injury to both horses and humans was too great. Furthermore, removal of foals alters the social and reproductive dynamics of natural

The Nature Conservancy intervened to save Carrot Island from development.

The lighthouse at Cape Lookout stands on Core Banks, across the inlet from Shackleford Banks.

horse behavior, and horse penning would trample the vegetation and disrupt the environment.

In 1994 officials from the Cape Lookout National Seashore held a series of public meetings and discussed these options with other interested groups at the North Carolina Maritime Museum in Beaufort. Surprisingly, over half of those present seemed to feel that the horses should be removed or, if permitted to remain, prevented from breeding and simply left to live out their natural life spans. After twenty or twenty-five years, the horses would be gone.

Ultimately, the Park Service decided to gather all the horses, test them for equine infectious anemia, destroy any positive reactors, and put a large number up for adoption. Mares returned to the island would receive annual contraceptive vaccines to limit fertility. With the birth rate in check, the population would never again exceed that which the island could comfortably sustain. The horses and their environment would be healthier.

As these plans began to take shape, local residents petitioned to block Park Service interference with the island herds. They asserted that the horses were in good flesh and the forage was plentiful enough to sustain virtually unlimited numbers. They attributed the die-offs on Carrot Island to dredge spoils deposited atop the largest watering hole. They sought federal or state funds for veterinary care of "snakebite" and "kidney colic"; for supervision of births; for medications, vaccines, hoof care, vitamins, minerals, and mare's-milk substitutes for orphaned foals; and for water holes dug with bulldozers. They suggested seeding the island to improve grazing.

Their protestations did not deter the National Park Service. In November 1996, the agency herded all 184 horses, considerably fewer than its original estimate, into pens. Seventy-six horses tested positive for equine infectious anemia. The Park Service released the 108 that tested negative after freeze branding large numerals on their rumps to make identification easier. (Freeze-branding involves applying a super-cooled instrument to the horse's skin, which kills the pigment cells without

An inquisitive young Shackleford stallion.

causing the tissue damage of hot branding. The shape of the brand eventually grows in as white hair.)

The National Park Service made plans to euthanize the diseased individuals. Local citizens were horrified. Many positive testers showed no outward sign of illness and appeared in robust good health. The Foundation for Shackleford Horses, a non-profit organization founded by local residents, proposed that the infected animals be isolated on Davis Ridge, a remote island-like hummock of 1,200 acres in Core Sound and Jarret Bay, connected to the mainland by marsh. Representatives from the Park Service, the state Department of Agriculture, and the North Carolina Horse Council investigated the site, but eventually rejected it due to lack of security for the horses and inaccessibility by state veterinarians who would need to check them periodically.

No other practicable options surfaced, and the North Carolina Department of Agriculture and the National Park Service decided to euthanize seventy-six horses. Their bodies were buried in a landfill.

A second roundup in March 1997 captured 103 horses. Five of these were positive for equine infectious anemia. The foundation was ready this time and had obtained prior approval for a quarantine site. The National Park Service gave these animals to the foundation, sparing them from destruction.

In 1998 President Bill Clinton signed a bill ensuring that 100 to 110 wild horses will be permitted to remain on Shackleford Banks, a number that should maintain enough genetic diversity for a healthy herd. The welfare of the Shackleford horses is now managed jointly by the Foundation for Shackleford Horses and the National Park Service, incorporating the expertise of veterinarians, biologists, scientists, politicians, and local citizens. The Park Service is responsible for ensuring that the horses have enough food and water and that they remain free from equine infectious anemia and other diseases. A roundup in 1999 confirmed that there were no more positive reactors, and so it is unlikely that these horses should ever contract the disease again.

The Humane Society of the United States says that in January 2000, mares from the Shackleford herd were given immunocontraceptive vaccines as a way to limit the herd's numbers humanely. (See chapter six for details about immunocontraception.) Horses may be removed from Shackleford if the number exceeds 110.

The Foundation for Shackleford Horses periodically uses volunteers for low-key "walking roundups" to corral the animals, then offers healthy surplus horses for adoption to approved homes. The foundation charges a six hundred-dollar adoption fee and imposes certain reasonable restrictions on how the horses can be used. This tale has a happy ending, because it appears that the horses of Shackleford will remain in a healthy balance with the island that has been their home for hundreds of years.

BONNIE S. URQUHART

Stallions don't expend calories nursing foals and tend to stay in better flesh than the mares.

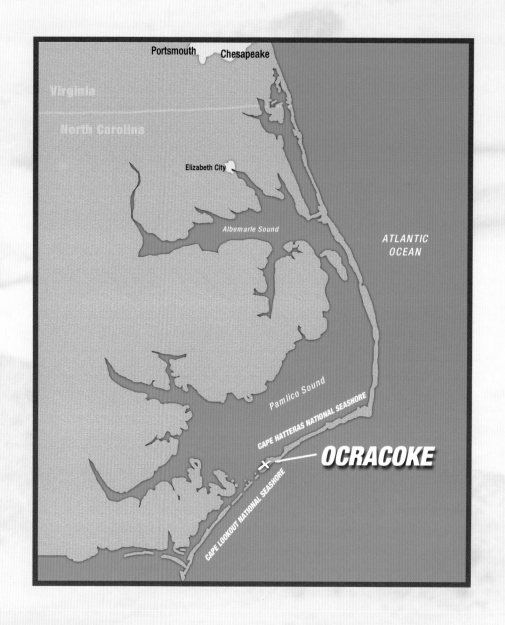

Chapter 4   BANKERS, BLACKBEARD, AND BOY SCOUTS

The origins of the horses of Ocracoke remain uncertain and the subject of various theories and legends.

BONNIE S. URQUHART

Chapter 4

BANKERS, BLACKBEARD, AND BOY SCOUTS

The handicapped-accessible Ocracoke Pony Pen allows virtually everyone a chance to get a close look at horses that descended from the herds that once roamed freely on the island. The Pony Pen is a popular stopping point and picnic site year-round for thousands of visitors. A brief synopsis of the horses' supposed origins stands mounted on a plaque in front of the paddock. As with all Banker horses, legends, theories, and a few definite facts vie to explain their history. Much is open to speculation.

Some, like Jeanetta Henning who researched the origin of the horses for her book *Conquistador's Legacy*, point to the colony of Lucas Vasquez de Ayllon as a source for the Ocracoke horses. In 1526 Ayllon established a settlement at the mouth of what he called the "River Jordan," which is believed by many to be the Cape Fear River of North Carolina. (The location of the settlement is widely disputed, and various sources place it anywhere from the Chesapeake region to Georgia.

For example, in 1992 *National Geographic* stated that Ayllon "planted a colony in what is now Georgia.") The Park Service puts Rio Jordan in South Carolina or Georgia.

Ayllon was a judge in Santo Domingo. He'd shown interest in the North American mainland as early as 1521, when he sent an expedition as far as the vicinity of Myrtle Beach, South Carolina, if the reported latitude is accurate (it probably isn't). He set out in July 1526 with some five hundred men, women, and children, including seventy to one hundred African slaves and several Dominican priests. His livestock included goats, hogs, chickens, and eighty to ninety horses. His first stop was the River Jordan, a body of water that flowed directly into the ocean. Both the Cape Fear River and Winyah Bay, South Carolina, fit this description.

Soon after, his flagship ran aground in the entrance to the river and was destroyed. He explored upriver but did not find a suitable settlement site, so he headed down the coast an estimated forty to fifty leagues, which could have been anywhere from forty to 150 miles because the length of a league varied. Someplace south of his original destination, he founded the settlement of San Miguel in a marshy area on the River Canaan. The natives refused to feed them, then turned hostile. The starving colonists fell sick, and the slaves rebelled. Ayllon died of a fever in October 1526. The weather turned brutally cold, and the survivors fled. About 150 made it back to Hispaniola (now the Dominican Republic).

Henning suggests that horses were left behind on North Carolina barrier islands after being released there to graze, safe from Indian theft. One argument was that their presence would be like living graffiti proclaiming "Spain was here" and likely to return and reclaim the land. But even if they did leave horses on islands, the mouth of the Cape Fear River is about 150 miles from Ocracoke, and Allyon's colony was undoubtedly well south of this. The mouths of the Pamlico or Neuse rivers would be somewhat convenient to Ocracoke, but records indicate that Ayllon's colony was by a river or estuary that emptied directly into the ocean or a major arm of the ocean. The Pamlico and Neuse do not fit this description. There are no horses at Cape Fear. There are no horses to the south until Cumberland Island and none to the north until Shackleford Banks. And why would starved, sick colonists travel hundreds of miles to place the stock on Ocracoke?

And why starve while horses graze in their midst? Other colonies were certainly not above eating their horses, and it is hard to believe that this one would starve rather than eat its horses. In Jamestown, Virginia, after all the cattle, hogs, and horses had been consumed, a few planters even ate an Indian (or several) during the Starving Time — one man even ate his wife, according to John Smith in *The Generall Historie of Virginia, New England and the Summer Isles*. If Allyon's colony did not eat its livestock, then Native Americans, who lived on some barrier islands and seasonally hunted on others, surely would have. In the early eighteenth century, stockmen on the northern Banks complained about Indians crossing Currituck Sound and poaching cattle.

None of the English settlers said a word about finding horses or goats or any other familiar livestock grazing in the marshes when they alighted. Thomas Harriot was the scientific adviser for the Lane colony of 1585. His *Briefe and True Report of the New Found Land of Virginia* was the first remotely scientific treatise on North America, and it influenced European thought and exploration for two centuries. In it he describes native animals and plants in detail, from the Carolina parakeet to cacti, but he never mentions horses.

In 1585 Sir Richard Grenville set sail for Roanoke

Island in command of a flotilla laden with colonists and the supplies they needed to survive in the New World. On the way, he lost one ship and then became separated from the rest. Upon stopping at Puerto Rico, he built a ship, reunited with one of his missing ships, and obtained horses, as illustrated in John White's watercolor of the fortified camp. Continuing to Hispaniola for more livestock, including additional horses, he captured two Spanish ships.

According to the log of the flotilla's flagship, *Tiger*, in David Quinn's *The Roanoke Voyages*, while in Hispaniola he traded for "horses, mares, kyne [cattle], buls, goates, swine, sheepe…and such like commodities of the island." Spanish accounts add calves and dogs. Evidently this was not enough to supply the expedition adequately. On September 3, 1585, Ralph Lane wrote, "if Virginia had but Horses and Kyne in some reasonable proportion…no realme in Christendome were comparable to it."

Grenville himself sailed on the *Tiger*, so he may have assigned the chore of transporting livestock to the larger or less prestigious vessels in the group. Unfortunately, his ship ran aground in Wococon (probably Ocracoke Inlet or its predecessor), necessitating repairs. Some writers suggest that some of the livestock thrown from the *Tiger* to lighten it escaped to run wild on the Banks. Documents do not mention livestock on the *Tiger*, however, and no other evidence supports this conclusion.

In the early 1950s Quinn compiled and annotated nearly all the known English and Spanish records of the Raleigh colonies in *The Roanoke Voyages*, which remains the standard work on the subject after nearly half a century. Even in this convenient form, the sixteenth-century sources are incomplete and often puzzling. They say little about livestock anywhere and almost nothing about horses in and around the Roanoke colony. It is natural to wonder what kinds and numbers of animals the colonists introduced and what happened to those animals during and after occupation. But the surviving documents do not support a great deal of speculation.

On Roanoke Island, under the leadership of Governor Ralph Lane, the 107 male colonists explored a lot of territory, inventoried a lot of natural resources, and antagonized a lot of Native Americans before the colony failed. The dense forests and malarial swamps of the interior were not very hospitable to horses, so the English did most of their exploring by boat or on foot. By late spring 1586, they were hungry. Lane had to send half his men to the Banks to live off oysters and roots and whatever else was available. Before the men succumbed to starvation and hostile natives, Sir Francis Drake arrived and eventually gave the remaining colonists a ride back to England. As in Ayllon's case, we can reasonably conclude that the starving settlers consumed the horses before the animals had the opportunity to establish a free-roaming population.

John White and his colony of English families established a settlement on Roanoke Island in 1587, when they were unceremoniously dumped there instead of at their stated destination on the Chesapeake. The birth of Virginia Dare, the first English child born in the New World, marked the increase of the village. But before long, supplies ran short, and Governor John White returned to England to bring over a shipment of goods to sustain the colony. Unfortunately, English politics and the Spanish Armada delayed White's return, and when he finally arrived, three years behind schedule, his colony was gone. The fate of the Lost Colony remains a mystery to this day.

The waters surrounding Ocracoke have long been a

The ancestors of this hardy horse participated in nineteenth century lifesaving missions.

challenge to sailors. Aptly referred to as the Graveyard of the Atlantic, the treacherous Diamond Shoals of Cape Hatteras extend up to ten miles into the sea. This is eastward enough to make land invisible to many mariners even in ideal conditions. Many a sailor thinking he was miles out to sea has run on the outer shoals without warning. The strong currents and extreme weather add to the difficulties. Southbound vessels were obligated to hug the coast in order to avoid fighting the Gulf Stream, and sometimes the passage between the Gulf Stream and the shoals was only a mile or two, leaving little margin for error. All other things being equal, vessels carrying livestock from Puerto Rico to Massachusetts, which could travel well east of the shoals, would have been much less likely to run aground or sink near land than vessels carrying manufactured goods from Massachusetts to South Carolina.

In the past few hundred years, more than six hundred losses have been recorded. The actual number is probably much higher. Before the nineteenth century, records are inconsistent and fragmentary. Wrecks were becoming commonplace, and people weren't always moved to write about them. Even the famous Union ironclad *Monitor* wrecked off Cape Hatteras in a storm.

A lot of ships carrying a lot of livestock passed by Cumberland, Assateague, and the Outer Banks on the way north in the seventeenth and eighteenth centuries, and there were probably undocumented shipwrecks of vessels containing horses. With so many wrecks and poor record keeping, it is quite possible that equine shipwreck survivors contributed their genes to the Banker herds, but we have no actual proof. Wrecks alone do not explain why horses are where they are and not in other places equally hazardous to maritime traffic.

Furthermore, Edmund Ruffin commented that horses turned loose among the Bankers often succumbed to the harsh conditions and the poor quality forage. In this century, tough Western Mustangs introduced to Assateague, an island farther to the north, died within the year (see chapter five). Even if shoaled ships did spill livestock, horses not acclimated to the Banks often perished.

In 1794 lighthouses began to appear along the Cape to minimize the loss of vessels. The Ocracoke Lighthouse has been in continuous operation since 1823, the second-longest unbroken run in the country. After 1874 lifesaving crews mounted on Banker horses or patrolling on foot monitored the beaches and struggled to rescue sailors from stormy seas. Stations were positioned at varying distances along the beach. Where they could, surfmen walked half the distance to the next station, turned a key in a clock or exchanged a token with another surfman, and then walked back, no matter whether nature offered biting raw wind, blazing heat, or hurricane. The more horrendous the storm, the more likely their services would be needed.

Unflappable, loyal, and sensible, Banker horses worked in partnership with the men of the Life Saving Service. These mounts were caught from the free-roaming stock that had long existed on the island and trained to haul lifeboats to and from the sea while nor'easters raged. They hauled equipment over the sand to shipwreck sites. The brave horses would stand in surging surf in the most violent tempests and wait while their riders rescued people from the waves. Some legends hold that many early Outer Banks settlers made a living off stripping shipwrecks for lumber and goods, but there is little evidence that this occurred on a regular basis.

During the 1700s, however, pirates, including Edward Teach, the infamous Blackbeard, used these isolated islands as hideouts, and Ocracoke Inlet provided plenty of cargo-laden ships to prey upon. The pirates ate the cattle and hogs that roamed their island hideouts. Some believe that pirates brought horses to Ocracoke as a source of mounts or even food if necessary, but no evidence supports this assertion. Besides, the herds were probably well established before the pirates frequented the island. Contrary to popular lore, most pirates were not native to the banks; the local population had little to do with piracy except in complaining about it and opposing it.

Pirates were not the only ones who tried to sustain themselves on meat stolen from the barrier islands. Stock was abundant and largely unguarded. Passing mariners of all nationalities frequently availed themselves of this source of sustenance. During the Revolutionary War and the War of 1812, the British Navy frequently ran out of provisions. Militia units on the Outer Banks tried to prevent the British from taking livestock but were not always successful.

Like the rest of the Outer Banks, Ocracoke was long used for grazing livestock. Surviving documents indicate the presence of livestock in the early eighteenth century. Immigrants undoubtedly mixed with the established herds. At various times, Hatteras and Ocracoke islands were connected, so their populations probably mingled. Because horses and cattle roamed the other parts of the banks beginning in the 1660s, it is likely they were established on Ocracoke long before records reflect their introduction.

Ocracoke appears on various 1500s maps as Wococon, Woccocock, or other similar-sounding variations. This is probably because the name was an Indian word, and it was spelled phonetically in map making. This seemed to give way to Occocock, also spelled various ways, and later to Occracoke. By the end of the colonial period, the only two sizable settlements on the Outer Banks were Ocracoke and Portsmouth. At that time, Ocracoke Inlet was the most important passage to the local shipping trade, and these two towns stood on either side of it. Portsmouth was founded in 1753, and by 1770 it was the largest settlement on the Outer Banks.

Livestock, including horses, roamed this island, too.

In an 1810 letter to the editor of the *Raleigh Star*, an unknown writer describing Portsmouth said, "Seven years ago an inhabitant of the Island of his own mark, Sheared 700 head of sheep — had between two hundred & fifty, & three hundred head of cattle & near as many horses...It is believed the Island at present is overstocked & much benefit would result from diminution of one third the present number." Forty-eight years later, Edmund Ruffin pointed out, "[T]he rearing of horses is a very profitable investment for the small amount of capital required for the business. There are some hundreds of horses, of the dwarfish native breed, on this part of the reef between Portsmouth and Beaufort harbor — ranging at large, and wild, (or untamed,) and continuing the race without any care of their numerous proprietors." Portsmouth farmers would attend roundups on Ocracoke and vice versa to acquire new individuals for their herds.

Ocracoke Inlet was a major trade route through the Outer Banks, but it was fairly shallow and treacherous, and most ships could not pass through without a pilot to help guide them. Some large or heavily laden ships could not pass through it at all. Portsmouth became a major port for lightering (temporarily removing cargo onto shallow-draft boats so that the large ships could ride over the bar and proceed through the inlet to ports such as Bath and Beaufort) and transshipment (moving cargo by boat between ships on opposite sides of the inlet).

In 1846 the same storm that carved both Hatteras and Oregon inlets demolished much of the town of Portsmouth. The new inlet at Hatteras was deeper for a while, and so the shipping business that kept Portsmouth prosperous shifted north. The population on Portsmouth Island declined from 685 in 1860 to seventeen in 1956. In 1971 the last two residents moved to the mainland. Today Portsmouth stands as a ghost town, complete with houses, church, lifesaving station, school, and cemeteries. It is listed on the National Register of Historic Places and is maintained by the Cape Lookout National Seashore.

Ocracoke Inlet is a wide, fast-moving stretch of water. Even crossing the inlet on a huge ferry burdened with numerous automobiles and passengers, one can feel the grab of current. Many small boats are incapable of navigating it. Yet on occasion a Banker horse sold from Ocracoke to Portsmouth would be so eager to return to its herd that it would actually swim successfully across the inlet.

In one well-documented instance, an Ocracoke horse named Old Jerry was sold onto Portsmouth Island and shortly thereafter was found grazing contentedly, back on Ocracoke. The horse had swum across one and a half miles of surging tidal current. Old Jerry also had a taste for straw hats, and he achieved notoriety by consuming tourists' beach hats left within his reach.

Every family on Ocracoke had at least one horse, and each of the free-roaming horses had at least a nominal/formal owner. But many, if not most, of Ocracoke's horses lived their lives, birth to death, running wild, breeding at will, handled by people only during the pony pennings.

The horses faced dangers in their wild existence. During one storm, the herd gathered at the tip of a peninsula. Floods cut off their escape, and every one drowned. Sometimes a pony would get stuck in a marsh, stranded until his herdmates rescued him by pushing him out of the mire.

Fourth of July pony pennings were a long-anticipated celebration, a festival of hard work and hard play for the Ocracokers and the visitors who came from all over to watch. Each Ocracoke family had its own brand, and foals were matched to mothers and emblazoned with an owner's logo. Banker horses were in demand on the mainland and were sold during these roundups.

They were said to be beautiful animals with long flowing manes and tails, easygoing, smooth-gaited, and relatively effortless to train. Gary Dunbar, in his 1958

An early twentieth century pony penning.

© NORTH CAROLINA MUSEUM OF HISTORY

book *Historical Geography of the North Carolina Outer Banks*, wrote, "The Ocracoke ponies are quite useful as a tourist attraction. Not to be classed with "banks ponies" and "tackies," these horses have recently been improved and are eminently photogenic." "Recently been improved" denotes addition of some outside genes — evidently non-Banker blood was added to the herd some time before this.

An Ocracoke horseman branding a foal.

Homer Howard, an acclaimed Ocracoke cowboy, was the son of Captain Jim Howard, who ran the Hatteras Inlet Lifesaving Station for many years. Homer and his Banker horse White Dandy were renowned for their ability to round up more than two hundred wild ponies without assistance.

He would begin at the north end of the island and work his way south, rounding up the various herds (which were understandably reluctant to proceed toward the pen). As they moved south, progress became more challenging as horses tried to detour into brush or into the marshes. Stallions from rival herds, hormones hot from the breeding season, did battle and tried to keep their mares away from the competition. Through sand-hills, creeks, marshes, thickets, and bogs, Homer Howard could drive those horses without any assistance.

Generally though, plenty of men were on hand for the roundup, and they swept through the ranges, herding horses together in one great drive — hundreds of horses damp with sweat and fighting among themselves in the scorching heat of July. Horse Pen Point was the destination for many years, though other locations were favored throughout the twentieth century.

Buyers sometimes preferred to have their horses ridden by the cowboys to accustom them to handling before their stressful shipment to the mainland. The riders obliged swiftly and effectively. They would chase a horse into an individual pen, crowd him against the

Traditionally, the roundup began July 3, when a handful of Ocracoke's skilled horsemen would ride north to the periphery of the wild herds that grazed in places with such fanciful names as Scrag Cedars, Great Swash, and Tar Hole Plains. The horsemen would camp overnight near the Sound, and in the morning the roundup would begin. They rode in McClellan saddles, a piece of military gear designed to be very comfortable for the horse but not especially easy on the rider.

rail, grasp his tail through the fence, tie his head to a post, and place a blindfold over his eyes. Then the men could work a saddle onto his back.

A cowboy would mount to take the ride. Off came the blindfold, and the horse was released. The frantic pony would run, buck, pivot, twist, and rear, but the tenacious cowboys were usually balanced in the saddle, and, therefore, could not be dislodged. At last the pony would decide that fighting was futile and realize having a man on his back was not such a bad thing.

Homer Howard was also celebrated for his skill in breaking the willful, powerful wild stallions that ruled the herds. Homer would slip between the mares and youngsters until he was close enough to vault onto the back of a stallion with a sudden leap. With one strong hand clamping off the airway just above the stallion's nostrils and the other hand clutching the pony's thick mane, Homer would stay aboard despite the stallion's indignant, infuriated bucking.

After about a half-hour, the stallion would admit defeat. At the first sign of submission, Homer Howard would release his grip. If the stallion resumed his battle, Homer would again cut off his wind. It did not take long for the stallion to realize that Homer would stop tormenting him as long as he tolerated a rider on his back. It was an exciting display to watch, and Homer Howard's stallion-breaking was often one of the highlights of pony penning.

Most of the time, though, Banker horses were trained in a gentler fashion, tempted with sweets, petting, and scratching the itchy spots. Sometimes the first mounting was accomplished in the Sound, with the horse belly-deep in water. This way, the horse's movements were restricted, and a thrown rider would meet with a soft landing. Horses gentled before riding was attempted often put up no resistance.

Shipping the horses off Ocracoke was not always easy. Ocracoke is thirty miles off the mainland, and the ponies had to be loaded and transported on flat barges, freight boats, and fishing boats. In one incident, two horses broke into the engine room of a fishing boat when a storm panicked them. Sometimes the animals would fall off the barges and drown.

It was no easier to make them feel at home away from their island habitat. They were accustomed to a diet of marsh grass and had to be acclimated to hay and grain slowly.

The ponies were pesky at times, but their presence was enjoyed by most of the Ocracokers. Hatteras Island had more villages, and people were less tolerant of livestock making themselves at home in their yards. Ocracoke Island had but one human settlement, at the south end of the island, and Ocracokers found it comfortable to coexist with the wild herds.

The ponies would often wander into town looking for handouts. One apparently developed a taste for fried fish and would reach his head into open windows to devour the family supper. The ponies would intrude into gardens and devour the vegetables if the gates were left open. Occasionally, a family would be awakened long before dawn by an odd noise only to find an itchy pony scratching himself on the corner of the house. Occasionally, a herd would stampede through town. But the horses generally were gentle neighbors and would not go out of their way to hurt a person.

In the early 1900s, locals thought that an infusion of outside blood would improve the herd genetically and add some height to the population. They also surmised that the fleet, maneuverable Banker horses would make superior polo ponies. Homer Howard's celebrated gray, White Dandy, was reportedly an Arabian from the mainland raised on Ocracoke.

In 1925 Beeswax, the son of the champion polo pony Christopher Columbus, was imported to Ocracoke Island for stud. Beeswax was not hardy enough to handle the rigors of barrier-island life, and he had to be penned and fed hay and grain. But his foals were popular, and most were sold to mainlanders for riding and polo.

In 1938 more spectators than ever flocked to the pony pennings to bid on these foals. At this time there were fewer than two hundred ponies on Ocracoke, half of them wild, the rest broken and trained. Jeanetta Henning maintains that the blood of Beeswax has been lost to Ocracoke over time, and none of his Thoroughbred genes remain in today's Banker herd.

The Coast Guard used Banker ponies to patrol the beaches during World War II. But the war years of the 1940s marked the beginning of the end of Ocracoke pony pennings. The wild ponies were left alone during the war years, and after the war, pony pennings were never as big or exciting. The number of ponies on the island was declining rapidly as well, from as many as four hundred in the 1800s to seventy in 1956, to an all-time low of nine individuals in 1976.

THE OCRACOKE ISLAND BOY SCOUT TROOP

Major Marvin Howard, son of Homer Howard, retired from his military career to his home on Ocracoke Island and organized the first and only mounted Boy Scout troop. Major Howard, who derived great satisfaction from working with both children and horses, founded Troop 290 in 1954, and most of the boys on the island enthusiastically joined. For the next decade, Howard served as Scoutmaster to about fourteen boys at a time and advised them in the care and training of their once-wild mounts.

For the freckle-faced, barefoot boys of Ocracoke, the Scout troop and the ponies were the focus of their lives. Each boy began by selecting a wild pony to catch, train,

The scouts of Troop 290 caught, trained, and rode their own horses.

and ride. Each pony, though living free, technically had an owner. Some were privately owned, and some were legally the property of the federal government. The price was fifty dollars per pony, a steep sum for a young boy on a remote island in the 1950s. Fortunately, jobs were available for any boy willing to work hard mowing lawns or assisting fishermen with the day's catch.

Usually two boys set out after the chosen pony, which had no desire to be captured. The herds evaded the boys at every turn, often venturing out into the water or the muddy marshes to escape. The preferred mount was a stallion, even though young stallions were the most difficult to capture and train. Stallions in general have four things on their minds — dominance, mating, looking out for predators or threats to the herd, and satisfying bodily needs such as hunger and thirst. Submitting to being ridden is not one of a stallion's priorities. Gelding a colt allows him to focus his attention on his rider's wishes and makes him more tractable. Most male horses are gelded young, but not the mounts of these boys.

It is a tribute to their skills as horsemen that they were able to ride these once-wild stallions bareback in a group. The feisty ponies were used to having their own way and often resisted domestication, especially at first. Stories abound among current residents. One time, so the tale goes, a rowdy stallion aptly named Little Teach bucked a scout from his back, kicking him in the head for emphasis. A vacationing doctor, in a slightly inebriated condition, successfully sewed up the scalp wound with forty-four stitches.

The Scouts followed many time-honored Ocracoke techniques of horse breaking, including mounting blindfolded horses as they stood belly-deep in the Sound. They experimented with filling an old pair of pants with sand and tying it around the pony so that he could expend his bucking energy on an inanimate object rather than a scout. Unfortunately, the ponies usually dislodged the pants and trampled them. The Scouts realized that it was best not to reinforce the trampling of that which was bucked off, for one of them could be the next victim!

Howard coached the boys in training methods and horsemanship, and they met most of their Scouting requirements on horseback. The boys also had the opportunity to show off their skills at the Pirates' Jamboree, which featured races and other tests of riding ability. Annually the troop would compete in the horse races held on the beach at Buxton and at Hatteras. This was no small undertaking.

The boys would set out early, for they had to ride a total of twenty-six miles to get there. To cross Hatteras Inlet, eighteen boys would lead their stallions onto the little ferry and hold them on the open deck for the forty-minute crossing, while the boat rocked and groaned underfoot, a situation that would panic most other horses. After the long ride to Buxton, the boys

would race in four quarter-mile heats, often besting stiff competition that included Arabians and Quarter Horses.

About five hundred to six hundred head of cattle still roamed Ocracoke Island during this period, and the scouts became skilled at cattle roundups and pony pennings, showing off their superb horsemanship skills for the benefit of the visitors. Branding was done with a hot iron. The fee for filing a brand with the County Register of Deeds was the same as it had been for two hundred years — ten cents.

The Scouts also helped around town and served as mounted honor guards for the Coast Guard. During the summer, the boys helped keep Ocracoke's mosquitoes at bay by spraying the marshes with insecticide. Astride sure-footed marsh ponies, they were able to penetrate the wide flats of muck far more easily than anyone else.

The Ocracoke mounted scouts often captured national attention. They were featured in *Boy's Life* magazine and in a children's novel titled *Wild Pony Island*, by Steven Meader.

Aside from the fifty-dollar investment to purchase the pony, no other expenses were necessary in maintaining their mounts. They could be released when not being used and caught later. They remained sleek and well fleshed on a diet of marsh grass. Most of the boys opted to build stalls in their backyards to keep their horses

Outside stallions periodically have been brought in to bolster the Ocracoke herd.

BONNIE S. URQUHART

close at hand, however. It cost about twelve dollars a month to feed and house a backyard pony, and the boys earned this just working odd jobs around town.

When the boys attempted to supplement their horses' diet with sweet feed, a tasty grain-and-molasses mixture that most horses relish, the ponies didn't know what to do with it. The boys initially had to place it in the ponies' mouths. Once the ponies noticed the sweet flavor, they realized that it was food. It was not long before they discovered the pleasure of other flavors as well. Many Scout ponies developed a taste for soft drinks.

The horses often had a close bond with their owners, and when set loose to run free would often visit them in the village when they wanted human companionship. Many learned to respond to the sound of their owner's whistle.

When Cape Hatteras National Seashore took over Ocracoke Island, it was a mixed blessing. The new status of national park would allow Ocracoke to remain wild and beautiful and would offer some protection against the condominiums and tourist attractions that have overtaken many East Coast beaches. But the National Park Service did not want free-roaming horses competing with the native wildlife it was charged with protecting. Cattle, pigs, sheep, and goats that roamed the island were removed by the late 1950s, and the Park Service saw no reason why horses should be treated any differently.

Ocracokers loved their horses. The residents asserted that the ponies were an important element of the island's character. Lawmakers argued that not enough was known about the horses' past to support claims that they had historical value. Emotions were high on both sides of the argument.

Major Howard put relentless energy into saving the Ocracoke horses. His family had been involved with Banker horses since the 1700s. His primary argument was the lack of juvenile delinquency on Ocracoke, which he saw as a direct result of involvement with the ponies.

When N.C. Highway 12 was opened on Ocracoke in 1957, the posted speed limit of fifty miles per hour posed a new danger to the horses. The scouts petitioned to fence a large pasture for the horses as a sort of a compromise — the horses would not roam entirely free anymore, but they would remain on the island to be enjoyed as a reminder of Ocracoke's bygone days.

The Park Service eventually granted a special-use permit and provided fence posts. Money for fencing was raised, along with the money for the first year of supplemental feeding. The state of North Carolina also contributed money toward the new lifestyle of the ponies for the first year. The animals were finally penned in 1959.

Fencing the herd was fairly easy, but getting them to stay fenced was a different story entirely. When the ponies wearied of confinement, they simply knocked over the posts and broke the wire. The Scouts would be released from school to recover the ponies and mend fences. The Scouts enjoyed this task — so much, in fact, that they would often sneak back to the pasture after dark and push over posts, ensuring another holiday from school.

In the mid-1960s the Boy Scouts of America demanded that the boys carry insurance if they were to persist in riding the horses in the name of Scouting. These children could not afford insurance, and without the support of the Scouts, the pony pasture grew too expensive to maintain. Ocracoke's mounted scout troop dismounted after only about ten years.

The Park Service took over management of the ponies in the late sixties. By this time, the herd was on the verge of extinction, having dwindled to a low of nine individuals in 1976. This rare breed was in danger of being lost entirely.

In 1973 Park Ranger Jim Henning was transferred to Ocracoke from Bodie (pronounced "body") Island. He took an interest in the magnificent herd stallion, also named Jim, and with his wife, Jeanetta, whole-heartedly devoted himself to the resurrection of the herd. The ponies were a sorry bunch when the Hennings first arrived. They were malnourished, full of parasites, and in dire need of veterinary care. Dr. Jasper Needham, a veterinarian on Hatteras Island, was brought in to vaccinate the animals, deworm them, and trim their hooves to resolve gait abnormalities.

Internal parasites are more of a problem for domestic horses than for their wild counterparts. Locals say the marsh grass diet serves as a natural wormer and is effective also for cattle. Most kinds of intestinal parasite are spread by manure. When horses are kept penned, they defecate in areas where others are likely to pick up worm eggs while grazing. Wild horses graze over a wider area, and manure is not encountered as frequently, although horses, especially foals, sometimes intentionally eat the droppings of other horses.

Chutes and pens were built to make veterinary care less of a rodeo event. Before the chutes were constructed, dewormer medication was given in a large trough mixed with food. The horses would compete over the offering. Often the dominant animals received too much; the subordinates, not enough. The chutes allowed dewormer to be administered in precise doses via oral syringes.

The horses had lost their fertility with the dwindling of the herd. In one five-year span, no foals were born at all. The last remaining Banker stallion was genetically incompatible with three of his mares. These three would deliver healthy foals, but antibodies in their colostrum, or first milk, would attack and destroy the newborn's red blood cells in a condition called neonatal isoerythrolysis. It was thought that this was the result of too much inbreeding. This assumption later proved to be false. According to equine geneticist Gus Cothran, blood type incompatibility is less likely in an inbred population, because the lack of genetic variability results in herds of very similar horses.

The Hennings saved three foals by bottle-feeding them, but something more had to be done. To save the herd from extinction, the Park Service brought in an Andalusian stallion named Cubanito. Modern Andalusians embody many of the same Spanish characteristics of the Banker horses and resemble the hors-

BONNIE S. URQUHART

A young visitor feeds horses through the fence.

es ridden by the Conquistadors. Cubanito was a handsome example of the breed.

Although bringing in outside blood resulted in live foals, the choice of Cubanito for this role has since been criticized. As it turns out, Cubanito carried both the genes necessary to perpetuate neonatal isoerythrolysis. When he was bred to the three problem mares, however, the resulting offspring were healthy and robust. The herd was on the increase again, but was no longer true to the original bloodlines.

According to Cothran, Andalusians, like Banker horses, are of Spanish bloodlines. But he writes, "the modern Andalusian is probably not directly related to the ancestors of the Ocracoke horses." The matings amounted to a crossbreeding, moving the genes of the Ocracoke herd away from the original lines. Several Ocracoke horses had been officially accepted by the Spanish Mustang registry, but Cubanito's foals were, as crossbreeds, ineligible for registration. Using a Banker stallion from Currituck Banks or Shackleford would have kept the lines closer to those that their defenders sought to preserve. (A 1991 study by Robin Goodloe, et al., states that genetic testing reveals that the Ocracoke horses genetically resemble Standardbred horses, trotters and pacers, a breed derived from Thoroughbreds and other strains.)

The Park Service also tried to bring in a horse named Sailor, who was born on Ocracoke and removed to Hatteras by Dale Burrus when the Service was selling off Ocracoke stock. The mares wanted nothing to do with Sailor. He did manage to sire three or four foals, all males, but he was never fully accepted by the mares.

In addition to the problem with genetic incompatibility, some of the mares simply were not conceiving. Hormone therapy was initiated in 1977, and subsequently three of the four problem mares foaled.

Adding to the effects of the dwindling natality rate, there was also at this time a run of sheer bad luck that befell the healthy foals. One died at birth. Three became sick and died from overeating. One punctured his foot, probably on a reed out in the marsh, as a newborn. His tendon contracted until he was walking on his fetlock rather than his hoof. He underwent surgery and was fitted with a cast, and he ultimately survived.

With veterinary care, the Banker herd began to recover. One mare reached the astonishing age of forty. That would be about 108 in human years. In her fortieth year she gave birth to a foal probably sired by Sailor. (Unlike women, whose fertility is finite, a mare is never too old to conceive.) She was unable to rise after the birth, but she lived another six months, hand-fed by the Hennings, until she finally expired.

Today the herd is managed at a steady twenty-five animals. They are larger than many Banker ponies, presumably because of the improved nutrition. Most stand between 14 and 15.2 hands at the withers (fifty-six to sixty-two inches tall) and weigh about a thousand pounds each. Visitors who return to Ocracoke annually take pleasure in watching the foals mature into adults. The boardwalk and viewing platform allow even the least adventurous tourist to observe and appreciate these animals.

Ocracoke remains an appealing Outer Banks village, all the more endearing for its inaccessibility. Most visitors arrive by ferry — the one from Hatteras is free. The National Park Service manages most of this island, and as a result it remains devoid of homes and businesses along the entire twelve-mile drive from the ferry to the village.

The Parks Service has protected Ocracoke from development and has preserved her natural beauty, but the island horses are no longer wild. The horses within Ocracoke's Pony Pen were born into captivity and raised on pasturage, supplemented by hay and grain. Breedings are carefully planned to maximize the gene pool. Stallions are kept in separate paddocks, and males not chosen for breeding are gelded. Some are trained for the Park Service personnel to ride on patrol or in parades. For all practical purposes, they live on a horse farm.

They remain on site as a memento of what was. Though no longer free to run the beaches in great numbers as their ancestors did for centuries, their confinement does not diminish their importance. The Pony Pen exists to preserve the last Ocracoke Bankers, survivors of a breed that nearly vanished, and the last vestige of an important aspect of Ocracoke's history.

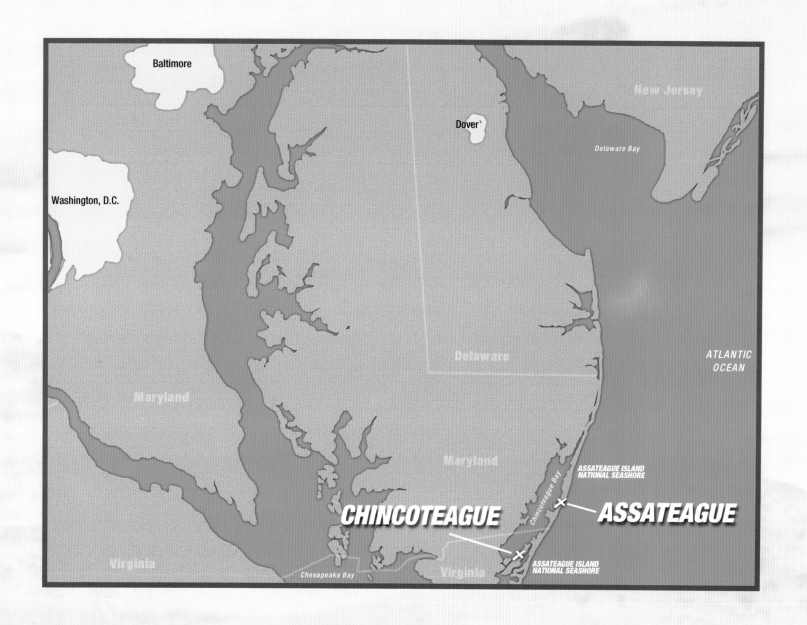

Baltimore

Washington, D.C.

Dover

Delaware Bay

New Jersey

ATLANTIC
OCEAN

Delaware

Maryland

Maryland

ASSATEAGUE ISLAND
NATIONAL SEASHORE

Chincoteague Bay

CHINCOTEAGUE

ASSATEAGUE

Virginia

Virginia

ASSATEAGUE ISLAND
NATIONAL SEASHORE

Chesapeake Bay

Chapter 5   SWIMMING THE CHANNEL

Assateague ponies swim across the channel to Chincoteague Island for the annual pony penning.

Chapter 5

SWIMMING THE CHANNEL

Chincoteague, a small island community on the Eastern Shore of Virginia, historically made its living from the sea. It has long been world famous for its oysters. In 1947 Marguerite Henry's book *Misty of Chincoteague* brought the tradition of island pony penning to the attention of children all over the world. Today the promise of both tasty seafood and a glimpse of wild ponies brings thousands of annual visitors to this unique little island.

Although festivals and activities take place in Chincoteague year-round, the biggest tourist attraction is the ponies, which live across the bay in the Chincoteague National Wildlife Refuge on Assateague Island. Every year public interest climaxes in a pony penning, swim, and auction that draws crowds in the tens of thousands and prompts national television coverage. The Chincoteague Volunteer Fire Company has maintained this tradition since 1925.

On the last Wednesday and Thursday of July, locals round up the ponies on their Assateague home ground, swim them across the channel to Chincoteague, and sell spring foals at auction. The proceeds help to maintain the herd and run the Chincoteague Volunteer Fire Company, which owns the ponies on the Virginia end of Assateague.

Pony penning is the culmination of the month-long Firemen's Carnival. Two or three days prior to the drive, firemen ride to Assateague on their own horses, round up the ponies that live on the Virginia end, and secure them in holding pens. On Wednesday the ponies are herded to the shore, where they wait for slack tide, the time of the least current. The Coast Guard fires a red starburst rocket into the air to signal the start. As thousands watch, the horses are herded into the channel for the quarter-mile swim to Chincoteague. The crossing takes only about seven minutes, but heavily pregnant mares and newborn foals are exempt.

The ponies emerge from the channel waters to spark

great excitement in the multitude of onlookers, who flock from all over the world to witness the event. Approximately 55,000 visitors pack the island each year. Countless others watch the event live on *Good Morning America* or on national news programs.

After a rest, the horses are driven through the streets to another set of holding pens. Any necessary veterinary care is performed, which is usually minimal, for the horses are on a regular schedule of immunizations, deworming, and other health maintenance — more veterinary attention than many domestic horses receive.

On Thursday the firemen auction off the spring foals and a few yearlings. Foals younger than three months are allowed to remain with their mothers after the sale,

Standing along the shoreline, Assateague stallions seek a respite from the heat and the insects.

BONNIE S. URQUHART

A young stallion enjoys a roll in the sand.

to be claimed in the fall by the buyers. In the late 1960s Chincoteague ponies sold for about $23.50 apiece. In the mid-1980s the National Chincoteague Pony Registry was founded. In 1994 a second registry, the Chincoteague Pony Association, was established. By that year the average price for a foal was $1,012.18, with a range from $400 to $2,200. Prices increase every year. In 1998 the average foal sold for over two thousand dollars, and the highest-priced pony was seven thousand dollars. This is more than the average fully trained purebred riding horse in many areas of the country. That year the pony sale raised $155,800.

It is thought that Assateague ponies descend from early domestic stock put out to graze.

Each year charitable individuals purchase several fillies for re-release on Assateague as breeding stock. This custom began after the Ash Wednesday storm in March 1962 that drowned many ponies. (Stormy, Misty's foal, was born during this storm.) Occasionally an exceptional colt is kept with the herd. In 1997 the only solid-black foal born on Chincoteague in anyone's memory was sold as a "turn-back," given the name Noah's Shadow, and released with the herd to sire generations of black offspring. In the past any unsold foals were also returned to the island — but in recent years every foal has sold easily.

Initially mares and foals are made frantic by the forced separation and whinny incessantly to each other. Many believe that it is heartless to separate a foal from its mother at such a young age. Indeed, in the wild, horses nurse for a year or even two. While early weaning is associated with increased mortality in foals living wild on barrier islands, it appears to have no adverse effect on the health of the foals bought at auction. Their buyers usually give them supplemental food designed to nourish foals, and many of the mainland-raised ponies grow far taller than their counterparts remaining on the island.

On Friday the remaining horses are driven back to Assateague. By the time the herd steps out of the water on Assateague, the mares have stopped looking for their foals, and they make no attempt to return to Chincoteague to retrieve them.

Many years ago, certain groups proclaimed the Chincoteague pony pennings blatantly abusive to the animals. Complaints — some justified, some exaggerated — were made that sick, dehydrated horses were being forced to make the swim. Day-old foals were being taken from their mothers and loaded into the backs of station wagons for lengthy drives to distant states. People ignorant of proper horse care and not equipped to maintain livestock would get caught up in the excitement and impulsively buy a foal because it was cute. It is not easy to raise a foal from undisciplined babyhood to become a reliable mount even under the best of circumstances, and these unprepared non-equestrians were clearly out of their depth, much to the foals' detriment.

Humane associations also disapproved of the "wild pony rides," traditionally held after the auction. Unbroken wild ponies, many of them lactating mares that had just lost a foal to the auction, were ridden rodeo style, bucking, wheeling, and frantic beneath contestants. This practice was halted in 1996.

It appears that many of the accounts of cruelty were exaggerated. Auctioneer Bernie Pleasants writes in his book *Chincoteague Pony Tales* that the stories about foals being transported in unsuitable conveyances are "myths," and that in his thirty years of auctioneering he has never seen anyone transport a pony in the back of a station wagon or in any other ill-suited vehicle. Humane

BONNIE S. URQUHART

Young "bachelor" stallions play fight. Later they will fight for real for their own harems.

organizations made a fuss over the use of bullwhips in rounding up the horses — but upon closer investigation, they found that they were being popped as noisemakers, not used to strike the ponies. And the firemen have generally acted in the best interest of the ponies.

The American Horse Protection Association stepped in, and now a full-time veterinary team closely tends the herd, assuring all ponies are free from infectious disease. State law requires that all horses be transported safely in an approved trailer. The Chincoteague Volunteer Fire Company also increased the size of the holding pens, added more watering troughs, and planted shade trees. Four times a year, the horses receive veterinary and farrier attention for immunizations, deworming, and hoof-trimmings. Even the burrs are removed from their manes!

The bestselling book *Misty of Chincoteague* remains very popular and is responsible for a good amount of the tourist traffic to Chincoteague each year. In 1961 the story became the successful movie *Misty*.

Misty was a real pony, born on the Beebe ranch and not on Assateague, like the Misty in the book. Marguerite Henry fell in love with the week-old Misty while visiting Chincoteague and bought her from Clarence Beebe for $150. Paul and Maureen Beebe, who inspired the characters by the same name in the book, halter-broke and gentled the pony during her stay on the Beebe ranch. When Misty was weaned, Henry had her shipped out to her home in Illinois to provide inspiration while she wrote her famous story. While the story line of Misty is not strictly factual, the setting is true to life and gives a fairly accurate portrayal of pony penning in the 1940s.

In 1957 Misty returned to the Beebe ranch to be bred. Her third and last foal, Stormy, was born in 1962, and in 1963 became the heroine of her own book, *Stormy, Misty's Foal*. Misty died in 1972 at the age of twenty-six.

Assateague Island is fortunate to have escaped the clutches of civilization, although man has left his mark in many places. The Wildlife Refuge is easily accessible to visitors. Many come to see wild ponies, but birdwatching is also popular. The lighthouse is open for climbing only on certain scheduled days each year, but the familiar red-and-white banded structure is fun to visit.

The ponies are abundant, not at all shy of visitors, and easily viewed from an observation platform or fences along the roadside. Barbed wire keeps them off the pavement and away from people. Separation is better for both ponies and visitors, but it does not always make it easy to see the ponies close up. Good photographs usually require a telephoto lens.

Deer drift like taupe shadows between grazing horses, which ignore them. Some of these are sika deer, actually a miniature Japanese elk imported to Assateague by the Boy Scouts in 1922. Others are the familiar white-tailed deer, smaller in stature than their cousins on the mainland. The deer are not very wary, especially at dawn and dusk when they are the most active.

People tapped Assateague's resources long before any records were kept. Before Europeans arrived, Indians of the Algonquian linguistic family used the island seasonally for hunting and fishing. The first recorded European to set foot on Maryland and Virginia was an Italian named Giovanni da Verrazzano, who sailed for the king of France in 1524. Historians believe that he landed on or in the vicinity of Assateague Island. He makes no mention of finding horses there.

Biologists such as Ronald Keiper believe that the majority of the ponies probably descend from domestic stock put there to graze. Early settlers to the

As winter descends, these Assateague ponies continue to carry good flesh.

BONNIE S. URQUHART

Assateague Island is fortunate to have escaped the clutches of civilization.

passed demanding that all livestock be fenced, and anyone who captured free-roaming livestock gained legal ownership of the animal. Putting animals to graze on barrier islands contained them effectively and also circumvented the tax on fences mentioned in earlier chapters.

In 1650 Colonel Daniel Jenifer obtained land grants to raise stock on Chincoteague and Assateague and hired about thirty men on Chincoteague and four on Assateague to care for the animals.

Virginia mainland imported farm animals from the Spanish ranches in the West Indies and let their livestock roam about town unfenced. Unfortunately, the animals did not differentiate between what they were supposed to eat and what was forbidden to them, and they often decimated crops planted to get the settlements through the winter. Free-range horses became such a nuisance that young men hunted them with dogs for sport.

As marauding livestock grew more vexing, laws were

Eventually small, short-lived settlements were built on Assateague, comprising families of the men who earned their livings from the sea, selling livestock, or following the establishment of lifesaving stations along the island in 1875, working for the U.S. Life Saving Service. Assateague Village was the largest of these settlements and at its peak supported just over two hundred people.

Here again, legends tell of Spanish shipwrecks that brought ponies to Assateague Island. As late as 1900,

Popes Island and Popes Bay were called Spanish Point and Spanish Bar by locals who claimed that in the 1500s a Spanish galleon wrecked here and the ponies swam ashore. Local legends perpetuate the Spanish story.

Spanish ships and pirate vessels are said to have run aground and spilled their riches here, and reports exist of gold coins found on the dunes. Whether or not these legends are true, the Life Saving Service

BONNIE S. URQUHART

It is unlikely that the foundation herd of Assateague arrived by way of shipwreck.

was kept busy by the many wrecks that succumbed to the offshore sandbars that bordered most barrier islands, as well as bad weather, illusory inlets, and other hazards.

Islanders profited from salvage from shipwrecks. Food, furniture, and other items were collected from the wrecks and kept, bartered, or sold. Many made a very good living from the numerous wrecks, and villages became efficient at dismantling ships that the

ocean had sent to them. This practice became a serious headache for officials in both Maryland and Virginia, who had difficulty enforcing the law on remote Assateague. In 1799 the Maryland General Assembly appointed a wreck-master to control shipwreck sites. He was authorized to command constables and captains of other boats in the area to cooperate or be fined. Anyone caught plundering a wrecked ship could be sentenced to death. Soon wreck looting was under control and no longer a convenient way for an islander to earn a living.

In the 1800s ponies throughout the world were used as draft animals in mines. Ponies were well suited to this task because of their small stature and great proportionate strength. (Compare the build of a draft horse and the build of a Shetland pony — the conformation is similar in spite of the size disparity.) These mines were dark, treacherous, and winding. Some sources claim that if a pony was blinded, its other senses would become more acute, and it would be better able to negotiate the mine tunnels. Blind ponies were also less likely to panic when lowered into a dark mine.

The Spanish colonized Central America and South America and set up mining operations there. Some accounts claim that they shipped in blind ponies to work the mines. A nineteenth-century document at the Baltimore Maritime Museum maintains that in 1820 a Spanish ship, the *San Lorenzo*, wrecked off Assateague en route to Spain, spilling ninety-five blinded ponies and riches from Peru and Panama. Don Pedro Murphy survived this wreck and declared that the ponies were on board when the ship wrecked. In 1826 Henry Lloyd surveyed Assateague for the state of Maryland and

noted in his journal the sighting of forty-five horses "no larger than a large hound." He added, " many appear to be blind."

Ronald Keiper, in his book *The Assateague Ponies*, states that park historians discount this story. And indeed, it would be hard to imagine that anyone would want to foot the expense and hassle of shipping a quantity of blind ponies across the Atlantic, when many of them were sure to perish en route. And even if the account proved correct, this would not have been the foundation stock for the herd — free-roaming horses had already been grazing there for well over a century by this time.

This is what millions of visitors come to see.

Although it is highly unlikely that the foundation herd of Assateague ponies arrived by way of shipwreck, additional horses may have arrived in this fashion over the years. One thing is certain: horses have been roaming free on Assateague for centuries.

The first lighthouse on Assateague was built and functioning in 1833. By 1852 officials decided that this original lighthouse was neither tall enough nor bright enough. The current red- and white-banded lighthouse that stands on the Virginia end of Assateague has been in operation since 1867.

Islanders grew produce in gardens fenced to keep the ponies, sheep, and other animals out. They harvested the maritime forest for firewood and building materials, used wool from free-roaming sheep, and raised hogs in pens.

Fish factories were built in Assateague Village to process fish into fertilizer and oil. During the 1700s and 1800s, salt was obtained by evaporating seawater at Assateague and elsewhere. Assateague Village wanted the state to fund the construction of a school, but to qualify for state funds, forty students had to be enrolled. Assateague residents satisfied this requirement in 1890

Outside bloodlines are apparent in this group's diversity.

by enrolling children as young as three. In 1919 a small church was added to the community — before this, religious services were held in the schoolhouse.

As pony penning has historically been an annual festivity in many barrier-island communities, so sheep penning was an annual spring rite on Assateague. The whole community participated, and afterward a feast was served over fires built on the sands.

Pony penning has been in practice on Assateague since before records were kept. The earliest accounts

BONNIE S. URQUHART

Salt-marsh cordgrass is the preferred diet of Assateague and Chincoteague horses.

tails that spoke of Spanish ancestry. Anyone who purchased marshland laid claim to any ponies living on it.

Scott's Ocean House, a resort hotel, was also established on the Maryland end of Assateague, probably in the late 1860s. It was immensely popular and attracted an affluent clientele who feasted on local seafood, visited the beach, and enjoyed the ballroom and bowling alley. Nearby Ocean City, north of Assateague in Maryland, attracted mostly locals while Scott's Ocean House drew visitors from as far away as Pennsylvania and West Virginia. In time, Ocean City added homes, hotels, cottages, and boarding houses and blossomed into a fashionable resort area. On the more remote Assateague, Scott's Ocean House remained popular until about 1900, when competition probably squeezed it out of business.

Waterfowl, abundant on Assateague, are nowhere near as numerous as they were before this century. This

date to the late 1600s. Toward the end of summer, men from all over would participate in the capture, branding, and sale of the ponies, and this tradition developed into a major event that drew crowds and spawned parties. These ponies were solid-colored — bays, blacks, and sorrels. They sported thick, often curly manes and reduction is in part due to the hobby of "egging," popular on Assateague as early as the eighteenth century. Parties would go egg-gathering on the islands and necks of Assateague, harvesting delicacies from the nests of seabirds. On Assateague and elsewhere, egrets, geese, and other birds were hunted ruthlessly for feathers sold to adorn women's hats.

Chincoteague harbored a population of year-round residents. In 1800 sixty people lived on the island, and by 1856 this number had swelled to almost one thousand.

The peak population on Assateague reached 225 around 1900. During the 1920s, one man, Samuel Fields, owned much of Assateague, Virginia, and would not allow others in the community access to the shellfish beds of Toms Cove. The residents then simply float-

BONNIE S. URQUHART

Ponies are familiar with high spots, where the wind blows more strongly.

ed their homes across the bay on barges and set up residence on Chincoteague.

Pony penning also became difficult with so much of the land privately owned. The locals established a single penning on Chincoteague for both islands. Initially the ponies were ferried across from Assateague by boat, but in 1925 locals began the tradition of swimming the horses across the channel, as is done today.

Chincoteague residents mostly made their living from the sea, and the island became world famous for the distinctively flavored oysters that grew there in great quantities. Islanders used oysters instead of money. Even today parking lots are paved with the ubiquitous oyster shells. Oyster shell was also the foundation for the original causeway extending from the mainland to Chincoteague. There was so much oyster thieving and squabbling over the valuable oyster beds that Chincoteaguers built watchtowers and hired guards.

Around the turn of the century, Chincoteague was still isolated from the mainland and had its own schools, a post office, and many homes, mostly made of wood. The streets were narrow, and the houses were close together. The people of Chincoteague feared fire because they knew that it could quickly wipe out their entire community.

BONNIE S. URQUHART

Separated from his band, a yearling stallion searches for his herdmates.

When a building was destroyed by fire early in the 1900s, residents recognized the need to purchase fire-fighting equipment and train a team how to use it. They bought a hand pump engine and, later, a gasoline engine. But when a serious fire struck in 1920, the town's people found that nobody had adequately maintained the equipment, and it would not work properly. Twelve homes and businesses were lost. Four years later, another fire took most of the buildings on the west side.

The Chincoteague residents vowed that this preventable tragedy would never recur. In May 1924, the Chincoteague Volunteer Fire Company was born. To raise money for fire equipment, the annual Firemen's Carnival was organized, and it included the roundup and auction of the Assateague ponies.

The Chincoteague Wildlife Refuge on Assateague was established in 1943 as a wintering area for migratory waterfowl. The development of wetlands and the black market for waterfowl feathers were pushing many species to the brink of extinction. The refuge protected nine thousand acres of coastal wetlands and wildlife.

Ironically, the Assateague horses that do not live in the wildlife refuge live a wilder existence. Although their fertility is artificially inhibited, they choose their own lives without the benefit of veterinary treatment or genetic "improvements."

No outside introductions of stock have been made to the Maryland herd since the National Park Service took over its management in 1965. According to the 1985 Assateague Feral Pony Management Plan, an Assateague landowner, Paul Bradley, owned most or all of the few remaining Maryland horses at this time. Keiper says that the Berlin, Maryland, Jaycees donated the twenty-one Assateague ponies to the Park Service to form the nucleus of the Maryland resident herd. The Park Service took over this herd in 1968. All the horses on the Maryland side of the island descend from this population.

The Virginia horses that live in the wildlife refuge receive regular veterinary and farrier care, and outside genes have been periodically added to alter or improve the bloodlines. Keiper mentions Shetland ponies intermixed with the herd to promote spotted coloration. He also writes that two buckskin Spanish Barb stallions donated by a restaurateur from Ohio influenced the bloodlines of the Chincoteague refuge herd.

In 1975 half the Chincoteague Refuge herd tested positive for equine infectious anemia, and affected individuals were destroyed three years later to halt the spread of the disease. In 1978 forty Mustangs were imported from California to revitalize the gene pool and rebuild the population. Food is abundant on Assateague but low in nutritional value, and the salty water and vicious biting insects are a formidable challenge to any horse. As hardy as these Mustangs were, they could not adapt to barrier island life, and most died within the first year. The survivors added their genes to the herd.

Officials from the Maryland Department of Agriculture and the National Park Service considered testing all of the Maryland population for equine infectious anemia and euthanizing positive reactors, but it would have been an enormous task to corral and test every individual. The tamer herds in the campgrounds would be easy to catch, but some of the shy, wilder herds would present a challenge. If they missed just one horse that carried the disease, the whole herd could be reinfected. To implement such a plan, they would have to be willing to shoot any animals that evaded capture in order to ensure that the disease was not spread.

The Park Service finally decided that it was not worth the effort. Because these animals are not sold to the mainland like the Virginia ponies, the presence of equine infectious anemia poses no risk to other horse populations. Fences prevent the intermingling of herds. In theory, flies could carry the disease from Maryland ponies to Virginia ponies, but, so far, there have been no problems.

In 1984 the National Park Service moved thirteen horses from the Maryland herd to the Virginia herd. These individuals were notorious for causing most of the difficulties with campers through aggression or property damage in their quest for human food. Virginia welcomed the influx of more fertile mares. All horses tested negative for equine infectious anemia before joining the Chincoteague herd.

Initially, the U.S. Fish and Wildlife Service was opposed to the ponies and saw them as a non-native nuisance that trampled vegetation and competed with the birds for forage. Fences were erected to restrict their range to five percent of the Virginia section. Almost all of this was salt marsh, which left them with plenty of food, but no way to escape the torment of insects and no high ground to climb in storms.

The Ash Wednesday Storm of 1962 flooded their grazing land, and twenty-two of the horses drowned. In 1965 the fences were removed, and the horses were permitted to range more freely.

Drowning still claims lives. A freak storm with high waves drowned twelve Assateague horses on the Maryland end in 1992. The biologist Jay Kirkpatrick says in his book *Into The Wind* that "something that can only be described as a small tidal wave" swept across the island, engulfing the animals. The storm waters were powerful enough to wash them across the bay and deposit their bodies on the mainland. Some bodies were even found caught in trees.

Another factor keeping the pony population in check is eastern equine encephalitis, a neurological disease that is transmitted from birds by mosquitoes. Kirkpatrick writes that during the summers of 1989 and 1990, almost forty Assateague ponies died of this disease. These years saw an uncharacteristically large mosquito population. The virus can be fatal to horses and humans.

BONNIE S. URQUHART

Ponies often will wade into the surf to escape the omnipresent flies.

In July and August, when the air is still and hot, Assateague horses take to the beach where the cool wind keeps the vicious biting insects at bay. Eventually the horses become hungry enough to venture inland to graze — only to be driven back to the shore by the insects. They move along briskly, distress showing plainly in their eyes as flies swarm and hundreds of engorged mosquitoes pattern their underbellies like tiny red beads.

Some species of birds opportunistically follow the pony bands and feast on the multitude of insects that they attract. Brown-headed cowbirds feed at their feet. Red-winged blackbirds perch on the ponies and pluck swollen mosquitoes from their coats or pull flies from between strands of matted mane. Cattle egrets tend to feed on insects stirred up by the movements of the ponies, but they do pick a significant number of ticks, flies, and lice off the ponies themselves.

The marshes are ideal breeding grounds for several species of mosquito, but the marshes are not necessary to ensure a large population of the insects. Mosquitoes can successfully breed larvae in water pools as small as a broken bottle or a fallen leaf. The dried eggs can survive for up to five years, and a moistening rainfall is enough to trigger their growth. They can hibernate as eggs, larvae, or adults to survive any season, including severe northern winters.

Drawn by the heat, moisture, and carbon dioxide released by warm-blooded species, mosquitoes are most active at dawn and dusk. In addition to the usual fly-swatting behaviors such as tail swishing, stomping, head shaking, and mutual grooming, ponies often wade out into the bay or even the ocean to escape the onslaught of the insects. Sometimes they wade out so far that only their heads can be seen.

More typically, the ponies wade into the bay until they find just the right spot, far enough from the shore to discourage flies, but still shallow enough to allow the foals to nurse — sometimes as far as a half-mile from shore!

Ponies are familiar with high spots where the wind blows more strongly and often congregate there when the insects are relentless. They also plunge into deep brush and rub against trees to dislodge the pests. Horses also have a "flyshaker" muscle over the shoulder area that can be constantly twitched to dislodge insects.

Although insecticide is generally not used in national parks to control pests, the Maryland State Park sprays for insects in the day-use area. Kirkpatrick writes that bands of ponies have been known to migrate six or seven miles to gain a respite from insect attack. In 2000 budget constraints precluded spraying, which might have caused an unusually large group of horses to mingle with tourists on the beach that summer.

Avoiding insects takes valuable time away from feeding, but the ponies have little choice. By 4 p.m., the air usually begins to cool, and the ponies again brave the marsh to feed. Salt-marsh cordgrass is their preferred food, as it is for most barrier-island horses. It is more abrasive than most other grasses, but it supplies more than half of their usual diet.

American beach grass supplies about twenty percent of their nourishment. Island horses also consume giant reed phragmites, salt meadow hay, and thorny sandburs and thistles, as well as rose hips and crab apples. In the winter, bayberry and elder twigs and branches become an important food source. Uncomplaining ponies munch greenbriar, a tough, rope-like vine studded with formidable thorns, as well as poison ivy. Sea lettuce tossed on the beach by ocean swells is an occasional high-protein treat.

A feral horse spends about seventeen hours a day grazing and produces between twenty-five and forty pounds of manure a day, depending upon food intake. Assateague horses have also adopted an interesting mechanism for reducing the amount of sand ingested with their food, sand that would otherwise contribute to excessive tooth wear and induce sand colic. These resourceful ponies often knock sand from the grass by striking it against bayberry branches! Kirkpatrick writes that almost all the Assateague horses employ this strategy, but most Western Mustangs do not, despite equally gritty food sources. Evidently this behavior is passed from horse to horse.

Ponies occasionally sip salt water, but do not drink it in large quantities, although they often drink the lower-salinity bay water. Small freshwater ponds are found on Assateague, but even these have some salt content. Assateague horses also dig for water and drink from makeshift holes in preference to freshwater ponds, even though they require much more effort. Kirkpatrick notes that he never observed them drinking from pools of fresh rainwater, even though this would contain virtually no salt at all.

The high salt content of their water and the crystallized salt on their food prompt them to drink twice as much water per day as a domestic horse, every three hours on average, a sharp contrast from the once-a-day watering of the Mustangs of the Western deserts. Water retention from excessive salt intake causes the round bellies characteristic of island horses. A certain amount of salt is beneficial — anyone who has seen the well-worn salt licks in the stalls of domestic horses knows that the equine craving for salt is a strong one.

The Chincoteague refuge herd differs markedly in composition from other feral horse herds because of human interference. The majority of foals are sold a few months after birth. More colts are sold than fillies, and some of the female foals return to the breeding herd every year. This results in a sex ratio of 4.6 mares for every stallion, nearly double the ratio seen in the unmanaged herd on the north end of the island.

The mean age of the Chincoteague herd is greater, too. Sixty percent of the Virginia horses are adults; less than forty percent were mature in the Maryland herd before birth-control methods were initiated (see chapter six).

The foaling rate is higher in Virginia as well. According to Kirkpatrick, in Maryland about forty-five percent of mature mares produced foals every year before the contraception program began. This figure is consistent with the average foaling rate in other wild horse populations. However, about seventy-five percent of Virginia mares foal each year. Kirkpatrick attributes the difference in natality rates to the fact that mares are less likely to ovulate when lactating, and the early wean- ing of Virginia foals encourages fertility. Human inter- vention and veterinary care also encourage conception.

High birth rates are seen as advantageous on the Chincoteague Wildlife Refuge. With the pony swim and auction attracting more visitors every year and foal prices steadily climbing, the sale of each new colt or filly will boost the Fire Company revenue. Every year is at least as exciting as the one before as more and more spectators pack tiny Chincoteague Island in hopes of glimpsing the feral ponies swimming across the chan- nel at slack tide.

Chapter 6  CAMPING WITH HORSES

Ponies and visitors sometimes get too close for comfort on Assateague Island.

CAMPING WITH HORSES

At the Maryland end of Assateague Island, visitors and free-roaming horses can get quite intimate. Too intimate. The seven-hundred-plus-pound animals troop across campsites, block access to bath houses, and tramp across beach towels. Bands of ponies unpredictably cross the main road, causing unsuspecting motorists to hit the brakes fast. Some ponies purposely block traffic to thrust enormous muzzles into open car windows, hoping for a taste of human food.

The Maryland half of Assateague Island became a national seashore in 1965, and the National Park Service took responsibility for the feral horse herd in 1968. Physically the Maryland horses resemble those on the Virginia section. A fence separates the herds, but sometimes Maryland horses have been transferred to the Virginia population.

The average height is only 12 to 13.2 hands, or forty-eight to fifty-two inches high at the withers. They are pony-sized to be sure, and the animals exhibit the unmistakable build of ponies — short legs, short backs, thick manes and tails, and that distinctive blocky muzzle common to many barrier island horses. Though the foundation stock was undoubtedly Spanish or Spanish-based, many outside genes have been introduced over the years. Over time, this blend has become a unique and relatively homogenous breed.

Apparently the Assateague horses of previous centuries were taller and built more like horses than ponies. Their small size today probably results from the interplay of many influences. According to Ronald Keiper, who studied the Assateague horses during the 1970s and '80s, Shetland ponies were introduced to the herd to promote pinto coloration in the 1920s. But genes are not solely responsible for their diminutive stature. Indeed, foals sold to the mainland from Chincoteague and fed more nutritious diets often outgrow their island brethren. Harsh environmental conditions and low-nutrient forage restrict growth. The feral horses of Sable Island, off the coast of Nova Scotia, however, endure far greater environmental challenges and remain larger in size. Sable Island horses also have different bloodlines that may predispose them to greater stature, even under adverse conditions.

Assateague horses remain round and robust even after a difficult winter. Carl Zimmerman, resource manager for the Assateague National Seashore, attributes their apparent good health to a combination of comparatively good nutrition and the use of birth control to limit the natality rate. Ponies in general tend to have efficient metabolisms and are usually "easy keepers" that stay plump on minimal forage.

Many of the Maryland horses have little fear of people. They brazenly wander right into the campsites in search of good grazing and any tidbits that they can beg from obliging humans. They walk under clotheslines and track sand across tarps while families work to pitch tents. They sniff and sometimes sample food cooking inches from open fires. Itchy foals view most human contraptions as potential scratching posts, from barbecue grills to truck bumpers. Campers shoo them away with the loud clanging of a spoon against a pot. The noise does not frighten them, but signals the animals that they are not welcome and should take their activities elsewhere.

Curious foals paw and chew tents. They tear large holes in screen houses and walk on in, even if there is nothing inside. On hot days, when the insects become intolerable, they cross the dune line to the open beach to stand at the waterline beside the bathers.

Many domestic horses have a far greater fear of human implements and toys than these supposedly wild ponies. Bright umbrellas flutter in the wind, screaming children race by them to the sea, and boogie boards wash up in the surf, yet the ponies seldom shy or spook.

Certainly a few tourists are bitten and kicked every year, and property damage does occur, but not nearly as often as one might expect. Much of this success record can be attributed to the vigilance of the park rangers.

Before no-petting rules were enforced, tourists would crowd around the animals, stroking them and braiding their manes. Even gentle horses can unintentionally inflict serious harm upon a human simply by kicking at a fly or a herdmate. A horse lashing out at another typically does not worry about the person in the middle. And even domestic horses have their moody days, showing their feelings with teeth and hooves.

The State Park Service and the Assateague National Seashore now preach that the horses are not to be fed, harassed, or petted. Doing any of the above will earn the transgressor a twenty-five-dollar fine on national seashore property, forty dollars on state park grounds. It is also unlawful to pull off the roadway to watch or photograph the horses. Pony-watchers must park in a designated area.

During 1983 one band of ponies was observed for 162 hours, and during that period was seen raiding campsites twenty-nine times in search of an easy meal. Now park employees making the rounds of campsites will remove food items left out where horses might try to get to them. Finding caches of human food reinforces marauding behavior.

Before this increased vigilance, horses would regularly open coolers and tear apart tents to find meals. Foals would learn these techniques from their herdmates at a young age. They knocked over trash cans and consumed everything from greasy paper towels to hot dogs. This bizarre diet disrupts the balance of a pony's intestinal flora and can cause colic. There is also little nutrition obtained from raids on human comestibles. Now, secure dumpsters have replaced the more vulnerable trash cans.

The State Park Service considers a pony a problem if it is involved in three or more documented incidents in one year that result in property damage or injury to a visitor. In March of 1984, thirteen animals targeted by staff as problem ponies were moved southward to the Chincoteague Wildlife Refuge. This action resulted in a dramatic reduction in complaints. If a pony becomes dangerously aggressive, the Park Service is prepared to "immediately dispatch the animal."

For about a week during the summer of 2000, up to seventy-five ponies (about half the Maryland herd) con-gregated in the Maryland State Park day-use area, occupying a quarter-mile stretch of beach alongside hundreds of bikini-clad bathers and screaming toddlers.

When asked why they took to the beach in such numbers, Maryland park ranger Rick Ward said, "They're wild animals. They have minds of their own. Some think they go to the water to cool off and get away from the flies, and the day-use area is just the best source of food out there...they're particularly fond of potato chips. They aren't dumb — they have even learned how to open coolers!"

The animals knocked over belongings, urinated on beach towels, and rolled in the sand beside sunbathers, but aside from begging food, were generally docile. The rangers concentrated on educating the visitors to avoid contact with the ponies and to keep food away from them. "Most of the time, the ponies and the visitors coexist peacefully. Very few people are a problem," Ward explained.

Ward also told of a couple who enthusiastically photographed their toddler walking underneath a stallion, unaware that if he had merely kicked at a fly, the little girl could have been killed. Ward says it might be a good idea to fence the horses away from the park visitors.

No matter how crowded the park might be, the horses attend to their equine activities unmindful of the audience. Stallions duel violently among parked vehicles and barbecue grills. Bachelor males chase each

The practice of feeding horses from cars encourages horses to stand in the road and risk being hit.

BONNIE S. URQUHART

other across campsites at a mad gallop. Stallions enthusiastically mate with mares in the shade of the bath houses while bystanders nearby pretend not to watch.

On Assateague the horses carry on the essentials of equine existence despite the presence of campers. But only a small part of the Maryland section of the barrier island is tourist-friendly, and many of the horses prefer to live in the areas not routinely frequented by people. These horses are more shy and reclusive than those that frequent the campgrounds. To the north beyond the camping area, Assateague is undeveloped and relatively unused. Only a very small percentage of visitors ever leave the civilized section. Consequently, much of this well-used park remains undisturbed and natural.

Free-roaming horses generally spend their time within an area known as their home range. Keiper writes that a home range on Assateague can cover 2.2 to 11.4 kilometers (1.3 to 7.1 miles). Ranges overlap at sites such as watering holes. When high-quality forage, water, shade, and other desirable features are readily available, the home range tends to be smaller. If their needs are met close to home, the horses do not need to go elsewhere.

Officially defined as a non-native species, the ponies of Assateague are tolerated by the Park Service, though not necessarily welcomed. The Assateague National Seashore and the Chincoteague National Wildlife Refuge are required to preserve only native species of flora and fauna, but the presence of the horses enhances the visitor appeal of the seashore. People enjoy seeing them, and many visit primarily to share their campsites with the ponies.

When Keiper conducted his research, he determined that a herd of 130 to 150 horses maintains a healthy balance with available forage and native wildlife. When he collected his initial data in 1979, only sixty horses lived on the Maryland section of the island. By 1994 they had multiplied to 165. In December 2000, the herd census was 175 individuals.

With the increasing numbers of horses came increasing interaction with tourists. In 1975 only three young bachelor stallions frequented the campgrounds. Eight years later, forty horses preferred to forage near the campgrounds. With more contact between horses and humans, more people were getting kicked and bitten, more private possessions were being damaged, and more horses were getting injured or killed on the road. Habituated to human doings, the ponies became bold and raided tents, screen houses, and garbage cans in search of food, scattering litter in the process.

Feral horse populations can increase rapidly, often out of proportion to the available forage. Equine biologist Jay Kirkpatrick says the average rate of increase for East Coast barrier island herds is ten percent to twenty percent per year. Free-roaming horses in general face no threats from predators other than man, and it is illegal to kill them. In the wild state, a mare generally bears her first foal at age three and may produce a new offspring every year until she dies at about age twenty. If half of her offspring are female, many of these will be foaling every year as well.

Disease, injury, age, and adverse environmental conditions claim some lives every year, but with losses only about five percent a year, they are not enough to balance the natality rate. Computer modeling predicts that, left to their own devices, the Assateague herd could swell to as many as 280 horses before starvation would begin to kill them off and limit fertility. Meanwhile, the environment would suffer catastrophic damage.

Clearly it is important to control the equine population on the Maryland end of Assateague, but restricting herd growth without imposing on the animals is diffi-

Assateague ponies routinely visit campsites. Some even know how to open coolers.

cult. Virginia's solution is the annual roundup and foal auction, which raises money for the Chincoteague Volunteer Fire Company and keeps the herds at acceptable numbers. The Park Service was not interested in adopting a similar program, fearing that it would cause injury to horses and humans and require expensive manpower.

In 1972 the Bureau of Land Management, which manages the welfare of the Western Mustangs, placed the problem in the laps of Kirkpatrick and fellow biologist John Turner. Their solution would be to develop some sort of birth control for feral horses. It was to take them nearly sixteen years to create a feasible method, but in 1988 they emerged victorious.

In 1988 Turner and Kirkpatrick collaborated with equine reproduction specialist Irwin Liu, who suggested they work on an immunocontraceptive derived from porcine zona pellucida, the transparent, non-cellular protein layer surrounding the egg cells and early embryos of mammals, pigs in this case. Sperm must pass through the zona pellucida in order to fertilize the egg, so it is an ideal target for immunocontraception.

This technology actually allowed researchers to vaccinate the mares against pregnancy. The PZP injection works by convincing the recipient's body to attack her own ova as a foreign substance. When researchers injected a mare with zona pellucida from pigs, it geared her immune system to attack the zona pellucida layer of

her own unfertilized eggs whenever she ovulated. This process blocks fertilization.

By April 1988, the vaccine was ready for field testing. Initially each mare received two injections of the vaccine, enough to prevent pregnancy for an entire breeding season. None of the vaccinated mares became pregnant that season. Since 1994 park officials have maintained contraception though a yearly booster, easily delivered via dart gun. One-dose booster shots display ninety percent effectiveness in preventing pregnancy.

The PZP vaccine is relatively non-invasive, non-traumatic, and well-controlled. It does not damage the environment and will not pass into the food chain after a mare's death. The Humane Society of the United States supports its use. Social order and behavior are not affected, and the mares do not appear to be harmed in any way by the vaccine.

The vaccine appears to be fully reversible in the short term — if the vaccines are stopped, the mare should regain fertility by the next breeding season.

In 1993 the Park Service decided to keep the birth rate on Assateague close to zero until the number of horses declined somewhat. Since then it has immunized nearly all mares over the age of two.

The equine population of Assateague has been extensively studied over recent decades, and the Park Service keeps records on the lineage and habits of each horse. This information allows biologists to determine which horses to dart to prevent genes from certain families from being lost from the gene pool. Researchers continue to spend plenty of time in the wilds of Assateague observing and documenting the feral herds.

The majority of visitors, meanwhile, do not venture beyond the developed areas of the park. This habit helps to preserve most of Assateague in its natural state.

But the emphasis was not always on keeping Assateague wild. In the late 1950s and early '60s, Assateague was the target for beach resort development. Over two thousand lots were surveyed to turn Assateague into a resort community, and over two hundred structures were constructed toward that goal. A sturdy paved road, Baltimore Boulevard, ran clear to

BONNIE S. URQUHART

Human food is not compatible with a horse's stomach though it doesn't seem to discourage some scavengers.

the Virginia line. Developers disturbed marshes to dig channels for mosquito control. Assateague was well on its way to becoming another Ocean City.

One obstacle to the sale of island real estate was that the only access was by ferry. Developers reasoned that a bridge across Sinepuxent Bay would boost sales and raise the value of the island homes. They began bridge construction by the ferry dock. Dredging up material from the marshes, they fashioned the causeway that is now Bayside Drive. But when money dried up, they were forced to discontinue the project.

Undaunted, they changed strategies. The developers donated a sizable tract of land to the state of Maryland to create Assateague State Park, expecting that the state would fund a bridge to allow visitors, and also land owners, easy access. Sure enough, construction of the Verrazzano Bridge was soon under way. Assateague was on its way to becoming another bustling resort city — until the Ash Wednesday Storm of 1962.

This powerful nor'easter destroyed almost every home on the island. Sheets of seawater literally picked up houses and dumped them in the marsh. The remains of eleven long-forgotten shipwrecks lay uncovered on the shore. Two new inlets cut through Assateague. Twenty-two feral horses on the Virginia end of Assateague died in the storm. Baltimore Boulevard was severely damaged, and to this day visitors can observe large broken chunks of roadway along the Life of the Dunes nature trail in the national seashore.

After this reality check, developers and homeowners alike wondered whether the barrier island was too unstable to support a resort community. Ideas to turn the whole island into a national seashore were revived.

Easy access to food has emboldened some horses.

BONNIE S. URQUHART

Looking both ways before crossing the street.

In 1965 the rest of the Maryland end of Assateague was designated a national seashore.

The Park Service is beginning to work with nature rather than restrict its action. In some areas, the National Park Service has let the high dune break down, allowing nature to take its course.

The winter nor'easters of 1998 did severe damage to the dune line, and many storms since then have worsened the problem. One can now view the ocean from any of the state park campsites, and most of the vegetation has been smothered under a tide of sand.

A mare takes no heed of traffic as she nurses her foal.

Assateague State Park began a major dune replenishment project in August 2001, involving all its own property and federal property at the north end of the island. Crews pumped sand from the ocean to create dunes about fourteen feet high, fenced at the bottom to keep horses and people off. The park planted the dunes with American beach grass, which will stabilize the new dunes with a sturdy network of roots. Crews also planned to move the dune line back to create a wider beach, but in the process were likely to encroach upon existing state park campsites and force the park to revise the layout of the camping area drastically. Funds have been allotted for yearly upkeep, and the project was expected to be complete by the beginning of the 2002 season.

Assateague is a very popular park in the summer, lying as it does within a half-day's drive of one-fifth of the United States population. Approximately two million visitors come to Assateague each year. As most of the visitors stay in the developed area, it is still easy to find empty beach and seclusion in nature if one is willing to hike a short distance.

Great beauty is everywhere in all seasons. The solitude provides opportunities for introspection, the ever-changing sameness of the sea is reassuring, and the wildness of the natural beach — and the horses — helps the receptive visitor reconnect with a world larger than an office and more majestic than the daily commute.

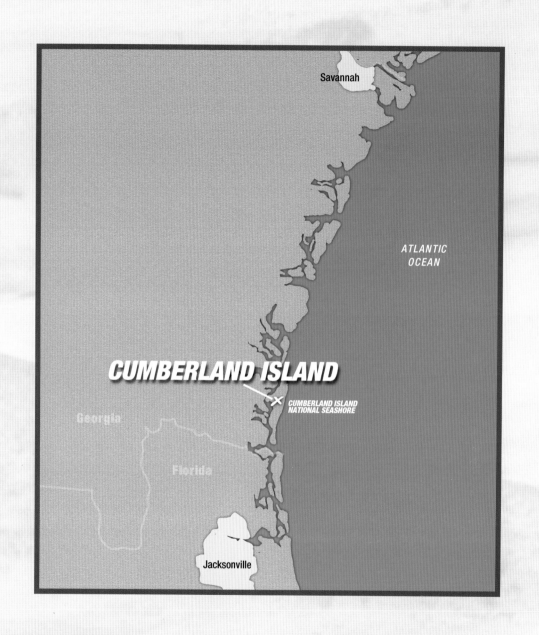

Savannah

ATLANTIC
OCEAN

CUMBERLAND ISLAND

CUMBERLAND ISLAND
NATIONAL SEASHORE

Georgia

Florida

Jacksonville

Chapter 7   HORSES OF THE TROPICAL WILDERNESS

Cumberland Island is a national seashore, and its equine inhabitants are afforded special protection.

Chapter 7

HORSES OF THE TROPICAL WILDERNESS

The late John F. Kennedy Jr. brought Cumberland Island to national attention in the fall of 1996 by marrying Carolyn Bessette in a quiet ceremony in an old slave church on the island, then retreating to the seclusion of Greyfield Inn on one of the last remaining privately owned sections of Cumberland. Few people outside Georgia had heard of this remote spot before the Kennedy wedding thrust it into the headlines. But it was once well known, especially among the wealthy and powerful, and had remained a point of interest to naturalists and nature lovers.

Cumberland Island, seventeen miles long and as much as three miles wide, is one of the largest undeveloped barrier islands in the world. Most of it is designated national seashore. Unlike the other American coastal islands roamed by feral horses, Cumberland is mostly lush, dense subtropical forest — one of the largest maritime forests found in the United States — and over 20,000 acres are designated wilderness areas. The forest remains dense despite extensive British and American harvesting of live oak for shipbuilding from the 1600s on. Live oak, draped in Spanish moss, grows prolifically in the steamy forests alongside palms and saw palmettos, magnolia, cedar, holly, pine, and myrtle.

White-tailed deer are smaller than they are in northern regions, and they prosper on Cumberland's abundant forage. They are small enough for bobcats to prey upon, and in 1989 these predators were reintroduced to maintain the balance. More than 323 species of birds are residents or seasonal visitors, including bald eagles, endangered piping plovers, and wood storks. An average of 177 loggerhead turtle nests are found here each year. Alligators lurk half-submerged in the shallows, river otters romp on the banks, and armadillos root in the rich humus of the forest.

Feral hogs remain a problem on Cumberland. They damage the environment and consume the eggs of ground-nesting birds and turtles. The National Park

Service would have gladly removed them long ago, but they are adept at evading capture and multiply prolifically, often producing four litters of six to ten per year. The current hunting and trapping regime has not made enough of a dent in the population, and the National Park Service is currently considering other hog-removal alternatives.

Cumberland Island has yielded some of the earliest known ceramics found in the New World, dating to four thousand years ago. The original settlers subsisted largely on seafood and wild game, and ceramic shards and numerous shell heaps throughout the island are among the few traces that they left. By the 1500s a Timucuan-speaking tribe, the Tacatacuru, inhabited the island and named it Missoe, their word for sassafras. Before Europeans exploited the New World, human impact on the island was probably minimal.

The first European to visit Cumberland was Jean Ribault, a Frenchman, in 1562. In 1566 the Spanish governor of Florida directed construction of a fort named San Pedro and then established the missions of San Pedro de Mocama and San Pedro y San Pablo de Porturibo to convert the natives to Christianity. Researchers believe that missionaries brought livestock to the island after this. The mission was abandoned after 1675, and about that time, the Tacatacuru also moved from the island.

In 1736 General James Oglethorpe, founder of the English colony of Georgia, established two English forts on the island. Spanish forces clashed unsuccessfully with English colonists at the southern fort in 1742, and Spain's defeat ended its incursions into the area of English Georgia. Following the battle, the island remained largely uninhabited until the 1760s, when England's acquisition of Florida removed Cumberland Island from the frontier and made land grants desirable. But before the American Revolution, few settled on Cumberland.

Cumberland's present name came about through the suggestion of an Indian boy named Toonahowie, who visited London with his uncle, Chief Tomochichi, and General Oglethorpe. Toonahowie struck a friendship with the thirteen-year-old son of King George II, Prince William Augustus, Duke of Cumberland. To seal the friendship, upon parting William gave Toonahowie a gold watch. Toonahowie, in turn, asked General Oglethorpe to name this island after the Duke of Cumberland. Fort Prince William, built on the southern end of the island, also honored the young duke, and Dungeness, originally constructed as Oglethorpe's hunting lodge, was named for the royal county seat in Kent. American soldiers were stationed on Cumberland Island along with their mounts during the Revolutionary War. At one point, provisions ran low, and the soldiers survived on a diet of "alligator meat, Madeira wine, and horseflesh."

After the war, General Nathanael Greene acquired Mulberry Grove plantation near Savannah. He later bought extensive property on Cumberland Island, intending to harvest live oak to sell for shipbuilding, and to build a home for his family on the site where Oglethorpe had maintained his hunting lodge, Dungeness. Greene wrote that in 1785, shortly after the war, at least two hundred horses and mules roamed the

Cumberland Island horses graze in the ruins of the Carnegie estate.

BONNIE S. URQUHART

BONNIE S. URQUHART

Pesky insects are ever-present on Cumberland Island.

island. (Robin Goodloe offers corroboration. In a 1991 article for the *Journal of Wildlife Management* she cites a 1788 letter from island resident Phineas Miller to Edward Rutledge that mentioned free-roaming horses.) Unfortunately, Greene died before he could begin to build or turn a profit.

In 1796 Greene's widow, Catherine, married Phineas Miller, her children's tutor, and they built a palatial mansion also named Dungeness. This building was magnificent. It rose to four stories and was surrounded by terraced gardens that grew many exotic foods. The Millers frequently held elegant parties, and Cumberland became a social hub for the affluent.

Prior to the Civil War, investors founded several large plantations on Cumberland, using African slaves to tend the lucrative Sea Island cotton crop under the scorching sun and supplementing the harvest with sales of timber, citrus fruit, and olives. Horses were necessary for working these plantations and for traversing the seventeen-mile length of the island.

Other island residents raised cotton and livestock. Census reports show the Robert Stafford family kept thirty to forty horses on its plantation between 1850 and 1870 despite the fact that most Cumberland Island horses were sold to help the Confederate effort during the Civil War.

When the Civil War began, the planters of Cumberland retreated to the mainland for safety. The families returned to find that Dungeness had burned to the ground, except its stone walls and chimneys.

A National Park Service publication, *Draft Environmental Assessment Alternatives for Managing the Feral Horse Herd on Cumberland Island*, reports that from 1800 to 1880, the Robert Stafford plantation sold "marsh tackies," small ponies captured from free-roaming island stock, for five dollars each. The publication also states that after the war, bands of "free men" came to the island to poach cattle and hogs.

By 1878 two hotels were operating on the northern end of Cumberland Island. Their popularity peaked in the 1890s and 1900s, but they shut down by 1920. In 1928 the Candler family, made wealthy by the Coca-Cola Company, purchased the land around the two hotels.

In the late 1800s the Andrew Carnegie family began to use the island as a family retreat. In 1881 Thomas Carnegie, Andrew's brother, bought most of the island for a winter home. He erected another Dungeness mansion on the site of the first, graced by verandas, turrets, and gables. Like the earlier Dungeness, this great house soon became a social center for the wealthy. Thomas and his wife, Lucy, welcomed guests, and there were plenty of activities for all, including hunting, fishing, golfing, and cruising aboard the Carnegie yacht, also named *Dungeness*.

The Carnegie estate included both carriage and plea-

Two bachelor stallions mirror each other as they graze next to thousands of live crabs.

sure horses, many stabled at Dungeness Mansion. From the 1880s through the 1950s, Appaloosas, Tennessee Walkers, retired circus horses, and Western Mustangs were all added at various times to improve the genetic variety of the Cumberland Island horses. Lucy Carnegie sold free-roaming hogs and horses to the mainland from the Stafford plantation. The Georgia State Archives document the buying and selling of many horses on Cumberland Island by the Carnegies.

Thomas Carnegie died in 1886, but Lucy went on to acquire ninety percent of Cumberland Island, turning it into a vast, self-sufficient family preserve staffed by about two hundred employees and including luxurious homes for four of her children. Lucy Carnegie set up a trust that protected the family's holdings until her last child died, in 1962. Dungeness was destroyed by fire in 1959.

By the 1960s developers were recognizing Cumberland's great potential as an upscale seaside resort. In 1968 three thousand acres of Cumberland were sold to Sea Pines Development Company, the same firm that turned Hilton Head Island, South Carolina, into a resort center. Carnegie and Candler descendants prized the natural beauty of the island, and together with a group of conservationists, they succeeded in blocking development. In 1971 most of the Carnegie property was sold or donated to the National Park Service, and in 1972 the island became a national seashore. The Park Service has not managed the feral

Lush vegetation makes for ideal grazing.

horses since the national seashore was established.

A small percentage of Cumberland Island remains privately owned. Only the thirty or so permanent residents are allowed to use cars on the island. To minimize human impact, the Cumberland Island National Seashore limits visitors to three hundred per day. The *Cumberland Queen*, run by the Park Service, ferries people back and forth to the island.

Most people want the Cumberland Island horses to roam free — with restrictions.

Feral horses have been documented on Cumberland Island since 1788, but it is unclear whether any descendants of the early lines remain. Incidental and planned introductions have taken place over the years, the most recent being the 1991 addition of four Arabian horses by a resident to "improve the conformation" of the free-roaming horses.

In 1991 Goodloe, et al., reported in the *Journal of Wildlife Management* that the Cumberland horses show the greatest genetic similarity to the Assateague herd of all the other East Coast feral populations, but also share genes with other breeds, including the Tennessee Walking Horse, Quarter Horse, Arabian, and Paso Fino. Kinship with the Assateague herd is difficult to see. In contrast with the short-legged, draft-like Assateague ponies, the Cumberland horses are much taller, longer-legged, and sleeker. While Assateague ponies are mostly pinto or sorrel, on Cumberland the typical coloration is appaloosa. Appaloosa patterns are rare or absent on the other barrier-island herds, but Cumberland horses display a wide spectrum of Appaloosa patterns: roan with white blankets, dark with white "snowflake" markings on the rump, bay with spotted blankets across the hindquarters, as well as other Appaloosa traits such as the tendency toward a sparse mane and tail, striped hooves, mottled skin, and a white sclera always visible around the eye.

According to the 1996 Feral Horse Management Plan, horse bands average 4.4 individuals on Cumberland Island, and each band claims a home range of about 650 to 1,062 acres. As in other locations, dominant stallions control harems, and dominant mares lead their bands to the best forage, the best water sources, and the best places to avoid insects.

Most foals on Cumberland Island are born between March and June, though literature from the Park Service says that mares can produce a foal at any time of the year. The breeding season is much shorter in the other East Coast herds than it is on Cumberland Island. Biologist Jay Kirkpatrick writes that the length of the breeding season appears to relate to the amount of time the herd has lived in a free-roaming state. The herds that have been feral the longest display the shortest breeding seasons. This is another indicator that the Cumberland horses have been free-roaming a comparatively short time.

According to the management plan, the horses of Cumberland usually consume five varieties of grasses. with salt-marsh cordgrass the primary item on the menu. Another twenty percent of their diet is consumed in the grassy forest understory, and they seasonally graze the sea oats and grasses on the dunes.

The first horse census on Cumberland Island, in 1981, counted 144 horses. By 1995 this number had grown to at least 239. The herd continues to grow by three percent a year. If this annual rate of increase is maintained, it will double in size by 2018. Decades ago,

How best to manage the Cumberland Island horses remains under discussion.

BONNIE S. URQUHART

the population of free-roaming horses was stable because of roundups and sales. Now breeding continues unchecked, and numbers have increased greatly, straining environmental resources. As on Assateague, Shackleford Banks, and Carrot Island, if the horses are allowed to multiply at this rate, they will eventually exceed the amount of available forage and begin to die from disease and starvation.

Some areas are little affected by grazing horses, while in others horses remove up to ninety-eight percent of the Spartina in the marsh. In the process of finding food, they trample other plants. This renders the marshes highly vulnerable to storm damage and erosion, alters the food web, and affects many other species. Plants are no longer in balance — dominant species are grazed into submission, subordinate species proliferate. Horses also may compete with native species for food and disrupt nesting shorebirds. Research indicates that if grazing pressures are reduced, the ecology would eventually resume its balance.

Livestock have grazed the Cumberland dunes for years, and as a result dunes are mostly flat and unstable. Changes in the dunes impact species such as loggerhead sea turtles and affect inland marshes used by alligators, birds, and otters. The horses are one of the remaining threats to dune stabilization efforts. (One might wonder which is more unnatural, grazing by exotic species or dune stabilization by contractors.)

Cattle were removed from the island many years ago, and boardwalks and restrictions to vehicular traffic have helped stabilizing plants to take root on the dunes. Park Service policy is to remove non-native animals that threaten the environment. Feral horses, however, have become a symbol of Cumberland Island National Seashore to many people, and so the Park Service has considered other options.

For several years the Park Service has been examining issues relevant to the management of the Cumberland Island wilderness, cultural resources, natural resources, interpretation, and commercial services. In regard to the feral horses, the Park Service has considered variations on three courses of action: remove all the horses from the island, manage the current population, or simply let nature take its course. Options included fencing a small population such as that on Ocracoke, castrating stallions, setting up an adoption program like Chincoteague's, or starting a PZP birth-control program similar to that on the Maryland end of Assateague.

The 1996 management plan stated that researchers at Princeton University were constructing a computer model based on the census and studies to understand the results of different approaches on the herd and the environment. The Park Service held informal meetings to allow the public and several interest groups to voice concerns and make suggestions. The Cumberland

Cumberland Island horses carry a diversity of bloodlines, including Mustang.

BONNIE S. URQUHART

Island National Seashore surveyed guests and considered letters and petitions received from individuals and groups. Most respondents preferred to allow the herd to remain free roaming — with certain restrictions. Technical experts, the Park Service, and the public all favored the plan to round up the herd, remove individuals for adoption, then geld some of the males and inject some of the remaining mares with PZP contraceptives — then allow them to roam free.

Alternatives are still under discussion. It is still undecided whether the horses should be confined to the south end of the island, where visitors can easily see and enjoy them, or be allowed to roam the wilderness areas, where they are seldom seen and do great damage. Reducing the number of horses will protect the island from overgrazing. The Park Service plans to keep individual mares on birth control no more than three years in a row to promote genetic diversity, if they opt for the contraception approach. Cumberland would use the protocols successfully adopted by Assateague for PZP birth control, striving to keep the population at 120 animals. Other versions of the plan allow only sixty horses. Private horse owners on Cumberland will not be allowed to let their horses run with the feral herds.

The least humane and most undesirable option would be to take no action — this would condone eventual starvation for many horses and major environmental damage to the island. This would be "natural," and it would cost nothing. Taking care of the results, however, could become very costly indeed.

A roundup and adoption program would rapidly reduce the herd to a number that is in harmony with the island. While corralled, the herd could be tested for disease before any members were removed to the mainland. In 1991 twenty horses died from Eastern equine encephalitis in the second recorded outbreak on Cumberland. It is also possible that some of the Cumberland horses carry equine infectious anemia (see chapter three).

The mission statement of the Cumberland Island National Seashore affirms that the agency is "dedicated to preserving the island's primitive character, natural processes, and the natural, cultural, historic, and wilderness resources, while offering visitors a feeling of isolation and wonder, and an opportunity to understand, learn about, and appreciate this island paradise." It is clear that wise management of the feral horses is essential to realizing these ideals.

Chapter 8   WHERE TO SEE EAST COAST FERAL HORSES

Horse watching is an activity that can be enjoyed by all.

WHERE TO SEE EAST COAST FERAL HORSES

Watching wild horses builds indelible memories. For those of us who spend too much time indoors juggling deadlines and commitments, hiking a fertile salt marsh and falling into the rhythms of tide and season, sunrise and sunset, are extremely therapeutic. Horse-watching is an activity that can be enjoyed by all — serious naturalists, adventurous hikers, impetuous children, time-challenged sightseers, even the physically impaired.

Active people with no physical limitations can get to any of the East Coast islands that support feral horse populations. Hiking, canoeing, and kayaking are available at most of these locations. Shackleford Banks and Carrot Island are accessible only by boat, and there are no bathrooms or fresh water sources. Cumberland Island limits public access and provides a ferry for a fee. Assateague offers both "wild" and "tame" camping options.

Those who cannot walk great distances, including small children and very pregnant women, can see the Ocracoke horses safely and with minimal effort from the handicapped-accessible boardwalk and viewing platform. Corolla Wild Horse Fund members sometimes maintain horses on the grounds of the Currituck Lighthouse. At the Maryland end of Assateague, ponies range all over, and it is usually easy to observe them. Assateague has paved roads that allow visitors to watch wildlife from their vehicles and trails to suit both the meek and the daring.

Wilds horses bite and kick, can spread disease, and are utterly unpredictable — observe them from a distance. Many areas impose fines for touching or feeding the horses.

Appropriate footwear is essential for anyone who decides to brave the backcountry in search of horses (or anything else). Hiking boots are best, but work boots or sneakers with good treads are acceptable. Hikers who plan to cover long distances should bring a blister kit.

Bare feet are not advisable — the sandy areas behind the dune line are studded with sandburs — round, prickly pods that are virtually unnoticeable until bare feet find them. Cacti, sandspurs, and thistle are similarly damaging, and the water harbors crabs, rays, and jellyfish. Barefoot hikers can sustain lacerations from sharp shells and broken bottles.

Hikers and campers should be prepared for the harshness of the barrier-island environment. The intense sunlight fries skin quickly, especially when reflected by sea and sand, and sunburn is a hazard even on cloudy days and in winter. Frequent applications of sunscreen with a high SPF can save a vacation.

The same mosquitoes and biting flies that torment the horses show no mercy on human victims. Mosquito activity peaks at dawn and dusk, but salt-marsh mosquitoes will bite even at midday. Long sleeves and pants provide some protection but are hard to tolerate when the thermometer is red. Insect repellent is essential. Ideally, hikers should wear long light-colored clothing and inspect themselves and one another regularly for ticks.

Hikers must carry adequate water and drink it often. Especially in summer it is easy to become dehydrated while hiking, and potable water sources are not usually available out in the wilder areas.

Poison ivy is an important food source for deer and ponies but is a bane to hikers and campers. All parts of the plant can cause a rash in all seasons. Poison ivy accidentally burned in a campfire can trigger a severe allergic reaction for anyone in contact with the smoke.

Swimming is refreshing, but the breakers can be hazardous, especially for those not familiar with them. Swimmers are frequently tumbled by the waves, sustaining sand abrasions, shoulder dislocations, and even broken necks. Riptides can pull a swimmer out to sea, and fighting the current, rather than swimming parallel to shore to escape it, can cause exhaustion and drowning.

When camping on barrier islands, tents should be anchored with extra-long stakes; the standard variety uproots easily from loose sand. Barrier islands can be windy. Improperly secured tents behave like giant kites and can soar great distances while unattended. Campers should also consider bringing a screen tent to provide blessed shade.

ASSATEAGUE ISLAND, MARYLAND

Assateague is conveniently situated within a half-day's drive of one-fifth of the U.S. population. Consequently, it is very heavily visited. Despite the high use, many areas remain remote and isolated, so solitude-seeking guests can enjoy the park as much as people who travel in packs.

There are countless recreational opportunities on Assateague. In summer beaches with lifeguards and bathhouses welcome swimmers and sunbathers. Anglers fish the surf spring through autumn. Hikers can trek though nineteen miles of wild seashore, and backcountry camping is allowed with permits. The Park Service offers properly equipped four-wheel drive vehicles access to fifteen miles of beach. Bike trails zigzag around the camping areas.

During the summer the Park Service rents both bicycles and canoes, and rangers lead programs that teach everything from birdwatching to shellfishing. Admission to the visitor center is free. It offers a touch tank, movies, information, and books about topics of interest — and air conditioning if you have been out on the beach too long.

For the less adventurous, Assateague National Seashore offers three half-mile nature trails among dunes, through forest, and over the marsh on a boardwalk. Interpretive guides are available for purchase at the visitor center.

Wildlife is everywhere, ready for observation and photography. Year-round, Assateague supports large populations of birds, both residents and seasonal migrants, as well as Sika deer, which are a variety of miniature Japanese elk, and native whitetail deer.

Red foxes live on Assateague, too, stalking voles and rabbits through the grass and slinking through the loblolly pine forests. They apparently have not made much of a dent in the rabbit population. As evening settles, cottontails emerge from the brush in great numbers to graze by campsites and roadsides, often almost under the horses' hooves. The endangered Delmarva fox squirrel is present in significant numbers on Assateague.

There are no poisonous snakes on Assateague. Hognose snakes feed mostly on toads and will hiss and threaten an intruder in a cobra-like stance. If anyone calls his bluff, he will probably play dead. Unfortunately, the non-poisonous hognose snake so closely resembles the poisonous copperhead that visitors often panic and kill them.

Deer ticks abound on Assateague, and some carry Lyme disease, so take extra care while walking through brush. Ronald Keiper writes that a pony-watcher can pick up forty to sixty ticks an hour.

Rabies has recently become a problem. Foxes, bats, and raccoons pose the greatest rabies risk, but any mammal can theoretically carry the disease, even a pony. This is another good reason to avoid contact with wildlife.

Camping options are many in the Maryland district of Assateague. The National Park Service offers year-round camping in seaside and bayside campgrounds. These are unreserved from mid-October through mid-May, and usually by reservation the rest of the year. Backcountry sites are offered to backpackers and canoeists, but campers must bring their own water supply, at least two quarts per person each day.

Assateague State Park provides day-use facilities and camping April through October. Whereas the National Park Service campsites supply cold (very cold!) showers and chemical toilets, State Park bathhouses offer hot showers and flush toilets. Food storage restrictions in both campgrounds are strictly enforced.

There are also many commercial campgrounds, motels, and restaurants on the nearby mainland. Ocean City, Maryland, is a twenty-minute drive from Assateague and offers many amenities and activities for vacationers who prefer a more stimulating environment.

For more information:
http://www.nps.gov/asis/
Assateague Island National Seashore

http://www.assateagueisland.com/
Assateague Island National Seashore Visitor Services

Adoption

Horse enthusiasts interested in adopting a wild pony that will remain free on the island should inquire at the National Park Service's Barrier Island Visitor Center. For a nominal contribution, one can pick out and officially name a free-roaming pony. Funds collected support the management of the herd.

CHINCOTEAGUE AND ASSATEAGUE, VIRGINIA

Chincoteague Island is bustling during the summer months, then relaxed and slow paced in winter. Many of the attractions are seasonal and close when cold weather arrives, but many bed-and-breakfasts, motels, and good restaurants remain open year-round. No matter how many visitors vacation on the island, Chincoteague manages to retain its quiet small-town charm.

The Chincoteague National Wildlife Refuge is open all year. Hikes at daybreak are ideal, although this timing corresponds with increased mosquito activity. The rewards, however, usually outweigh the loss of blood. Human traffic is minimal, wildlife is active, and sunrise over the Atlantic can be unforgettable. While the ponies can appear just about anywhere on Assateague, on the refuge they are most commonly spotted in the marshes on the south side of the main road. Barbed-wire fences keep the ponies off the roads of the refuge and prevent people from feeding them. The observation platform on the Woodland Trail is often a good vantage point.

Deer are so abundant at dawn and dusk that one can easily spot more than a dozen an hour. They are well camouflaged in the salt marsh, however.

Pets are prohibited on the refuge, even inside a vehicle. Camping is not allowed in the Virginia district of Assateague Island, but there are many popular commercial campgrounds on Chincoteague, as well as comfortable motels and bed-and-breakfasts. The Toms Cove Visitor Center within the refuge operates year-round, but ranger-led programs are only offered in the summer. The Coast Guard opens the Assateague Lighthouse for climbing one weekend each month from May through November.

The annual Firemen's Carnival lasts the entire month of July, and the Pony Swim and Auction is always held on the last Wednesday and Thursday of the month. Chincoteague is home to many talented artists and woodcarvers, and shops offer a wide selection of decoys and bird art. The active visitor can bicycle the scenic backroads of Chincoteague or the refuge, dive on shipwrecks offshore, or rent a kayak to catch glimpses of shy waterfowl and other wildlife.

For more information:
http://www.chincoteaguechamber.com/
The Chincoteague Chamber of Commerce has a great site and lots of information.

Adoption

Ponies can be adopted at Pony Penning the last week in July every year.

COROLLA, NORTH CAROLINA

Corolla has become a prime vacation spot for the affluent. Multimillion-dollar seasonal homes cluster prominently throughout the village and amenities attract wealthy vacationers from all over the world. North of the village in the Currituck National Wildlife Refuge, natural processes continue largely undisturbed. Storms sculpt the high dunes into erratic shapes patterned with the lacy impressions of wind-whipped grass, while overwash erodes ravines and gullies. In the heat of summer, the free-roaming horses often venture out to the beach to escape the insects and to cool off in the sea breeze.

Visitors who hike the beach north of Corolla are not always lucky enough to spot wild horses. Four-wheel-drive safaris take visitors into the heart of the Wildlife Refuge for a closer look at them, and guides usually know the whereabouts of the bands. Visitors can also check at the Currituck Lighthouse complex — horses sometime live there in corrals. The 150-foot red brick structure is open seasonally for climbing, and the Keepers' House, which now functions as a museum shop, is open daily March through Thanksgiving weekend.

There is plenty to do in Corolla. Besides swimming and sunning, many visitors enjoy four-wheeling or windsurfing, parasailing, jet skiing, sailing, fishing, kayaking, canoeing, and other water sports. Farther south on the Outer Banks, one can hang-glide on Jockeys Ridge or observe dolphins from small boats. The less enterprising can explore the many unique shops in the area.

For more information:
http://www.corollawildhorses.com/

The Corolla Wild Horse Fund has a great website. The historical page has some inaccuracies, but the rest is visually appealing and very informative.

Adoption

The Corolla Wild Horse Fund is responsible for many aspects of the current management plan, including health inspection, population control, record keeping, and census taking. It is also responsible for educational materials and programs, repairing the fence and cattle guard, and maintaining a trailer to haul the horses back to the refuge when they stray.

The Corolla Wild Horse Fund greatly appreciates donations of any amount. It costs thirty-five dollars to adopt a free-roaming Corolla wild horse. This entitles the adopter to a five-by-seven-inch color photo of the horse, an adoption certificate, and a Corolla Wild Horse bumper sticker. More important, adopters gain the satisfaction of helping the Corolla Wild Horse Fund preserve the wild horses of Currituck Banks.

For more information:
Corolla Wild Horse Fund, P.O. Box 361,
Corolla, NC 27927; (252) 453-8152

SHACKLEFORD BANKS AND CARROT ISLAND, NORTH CAROLINA

It is entirely possible to spend a day or two on Shackleford at peak season and see no other people except those out in the sound on boats. Carrot Island is less remote, situated across a narrow waterway from the Beaufort waterfront, yet natural and largely undisturbed.

Both islands offer no buildings, bathrooms, or fresh water except for one spigot at the ferry landing at the west side of Shackleford. Hikers and campers must pack in their own water. Visitors will need insect repellent, sunscreen, food, good walking shoes, and a hat.

The mosquitoes are enormous on Shackleford Banks. They are tolerable on windy days, but when the air is still, they rise up from the marsh and descend like a black veil upon any warm-blooded creature that presents itself. Multiple applications of sophisticated repellents do not seem to faze them, and they can even bite though thick clothing. Even as late as October, sometimes the best strategy is to retreat to a tent and wait for the wind to start blowing again.

Feral horses are abundant, and a hiker's chances of seeing them are good. Primitive camping is permitted anywhere on Shackleford. There are neither designated campsites nor garbage cans, and campers should make an effort to leave nothing behind. Campfires are allowed below the high-tide line, but firewood is scarce and the Park Service recommends using a camp stove.

Numerous businesses on Harkers Island and in Beaufort provide ferry service to Shackleford Banks and Carrot Island, as well as guided nature tours and kayaking trips. The National Park Service's Visitor Center on Harkers Island is open daily year-round.

For more information:
Foundation for Shackleford Horses Inc., P.O. Box 841,
Beaufort, NC 28516
http://www.shacklefordhorses.org

Adoption

Occasionally, the Foundation for Shackleford Horses conducts roundups and allows the public to adopt horses and take them to the mainland. For more information, contact the foundation.

A great account of the 1999 roundup is at http://www.kbrhorse.net/wclo/shackr01.html

---

OCRACOKE, NORTH CAROLINA

Barrier islands are always new, constantly shifted and rearranged by the elements, yet a feeling of timelessness awaits the visitor who hikes beyond the developed areas of Ocracoke. One can stand on a dune and imagine oneself removed a century or two in time, surrounded by hundreds of free-roaming horses and cows beyond the next hillock. It is possible to stroll for hours on the Ocracoke beach in July and not encounter another soul.

In summer the island's nature trails are best visited on windy days when the insects are not as active. Ferocious mosquitoes and biting flies can chase the most tenacious hikers out of the woods despite liberal use of the strongest insect repellent. (A popular T-shirt sold in the local variety store features an enormous mosquito and proclaims "I gave blood on Ocracoke.")

The Ocracoke Pony Pen is a roadside exhibit area on N.C. Highway 12 about five miles north of Ocracoke Village. It includes a handicapped-accessible boardwalk, viewing platforms, and a picnic area. There is no fee. It is hard to resist petting the horses in the compound when they come to the fence and push hungry muzzles hopefully at pockets. But pony-watchers should respect the Park Service's efforts to separate ponies from people and refrain from petting or feeding them.

Fishing and beach driving are popular activities, and boat charters and rentals are available in the harbor area. The lifeguarded beach is open from early June into late August. Picturesque Ocracoke Village, listed on the National Register of Historic Places in 1990, offers unique shops and restaurants, and the quiet side streets are ideal for strolling and bicycling. The 1823 Ocracoke Lighthouse is not open for climbing, but the grounds are open to the public. Kayak ecotours familiarize vacationers with life in the quiet marshes, and private stables offer horseback riding by reservation.

Several businesses offer twenty-minute boat rides to Portsmouth Village, the historic barrier island ghost town. The U.S. Life Saving Station, Methodist Church, U.S. Postal Service and General Store, and Village Visitor Center are open to the public. Portsmouth was once the largest settlement on the Outer Banks, but was gradually abandoned. In 1976 it became part of the Cape Lookout National Seashore.

The free Hatteras Inlet ferry brings in the majority of vacationers, and toll ferries transport passengers and their vehicles to and from Swan Quarter, on the mainland, and Cedar Island. The ferry ride is exciting for children and often for adults as well. Sometimes one can glimpse a dolphin or two, and children delight in hurling chunks of bread to the swirling, squabbling flocks of gulls that follow the boat.

Sites in the Park Service campground on Ocracoke are available by reservation. It has modern restrooms, potable water, grills, tables, and unheated showers, but no utility connections or shade trees. There are also private campgrounds on the island, as well as motels and vacation-cottage rentals.

Information about Ocracoke and the rest of the Cape Hatteras National Seashore can be found at http://www.nps.gov/caha/

Cumberland Island, Georgia

Visitors to Cumberland Island often find the lack of human noise and activity disorienting. The Park Service limits access, and with so little human interference, the wilderness areas remain quite wild. Only fit and robust campers should attempt long stays in the backcountry. Energetic hikers can explore over fifty miles of hiking trails and miles of wide, sandy beach.

Cumberland supports diverse ecosystems including sand dunes, freshwater swamp, marsh, and dense forest. Butterflies are everywhere. Live oaks crook their limbs around colonies of epiphytes as if to protect them from the horses and deer feeding below. The air is busy with the sounds of birds and insects and the clacking of palmettos in the breeze.

Male rufous-sided towhees sing rivals away in a different dialect than they do in the Northeast. In New England the phonetic representation of their song is "Drink Your Tea!" At Cape Hatteras, the tune is "Y'all drink your tea!" In Georgia, towhees add an extra note or two, and the rhythm is dreamy and languorous: "Drink someone's tea. Drink everyone's tea." They are so territorial they have been known to do battle with their reflections in car mirrors, screaming "SheWeeenk!" and angrily pecking at the glass.

Horse-watchers should ask personnel at the visitor center about optimal viewing locations. Currently the National Park Service is considering herd management options, including confining horses to specific areas. Many of these horses have no fear of humans and are easy to approach, but the Park Service requests that visitors refrain from feeding or interacting with them.

Ferry reservations to the park are required. Cumberland Island is seven miles east of St. Marys, Georgia, and a private passenger ferry takes visitors on the forty-five-minute trip to the national seashore. The ferry does not transport bicycles or cars. Guests who miss the ferry must make private arrangements for transportation. Charter boats in St. Marys are an alternative and are more flexible about arrivals and departures and what visitors may bring. Sometimes manatees can be glimpsed from the ferry docks.

A good hike for day-trippers is the 3.5-mile loop starting at Dungeness Dock. This trail continues by Dungeness mansion and past the cemetery where the tombstone of Revolutionary War hero Lighthorse Harry Lee is located. Within the live oaks around the Dungeness ruins stands the oldest structure on Cumberland Island, an 1800s gardener's cottage converted by the Carnegies into an office building. From there, the trail spills over the dunes to a wide, white sand beach, then continues to the National Park Service's Sea Camp Campground.

Camping on Cumberland can be very challenging. Campers must reserve their sites well in advance, choosing between one developed and four primitive backcountry camping areas. Overnight visitation is restricted to 120 campers, and the maximum stay is seven days. The developed campground at Sea Camp offers toilets, cold showers, drinking water, grills, fire rings, and picnic tables. The backcountry sites are 3.5 to 10.8 miles from the ferry dock and have no facilities, not even fresh water.

There are no stores or services, so visitors must bring everything they need. Strict leave-no-trace policies necessitate packing all trash off the island.

The island is very hot and humid from May though September. In summer insects can be ferocious, especially on windless days. In the backcountry, poisonous cottonmouth snakes are not uncommon in areas near water. Backwoods hikers should pack snakebite kits and know how to use them, for help is not always at hand.

On the mainland the town of St. Marys offers lodging and campgrounds for people who are not keen about staying in the remoteness of Cumberland. A less taxing plan is to stay in St. Marys, take the ferry to the island to explore by day, then come back to enjoy the restaurants, stores, and amenities on the mainland.

The historic Greyfield Inn is the one luxurious vacation destination on Cumberland Island. Built in 1900, it offers fine dining, expensive rooms, and even on-site naturalists to provide tours of the island to guests.

For more information:
http://www.stmaryswelcome.com

The Park Service is currently considering management options. One possibility is a round-up and adoption. Contact the National Park Service for more information.
http://www.nps.gov/cuis

For more information about the horses of *Hoofprints in the Sand*, please visit *www.feralhorse.com*

Conclusion

GUARDIANS OF
THE HERDS

Horses mean something to us and to remove them entirely would rob us of a valuable cultural resource. We cannot overlook the fact that horses touch our souls in ways that few other species can. Even people who have never been close to a horse can marvel at its innate grace and beauty. Horses are symbols of power, elegance, and freedom. Books like *The Horse Whisperer* resonate within a broad array of human hearts. Classics such as *Black Beauty*, *National Velvet*, *Misty of Chincoteague*, and *The Black Stallion* remain popular with children generation after generation, while the Saddle Club series speaks to the most recent crop of wide-eyed, horse-hungry youngsters who regularly weave horses into their fantasies.

Historian Wynne Dough, curator of the Outer Banks History Center from its creation in 1988 to 2000, agrees that the horses should be preserved, but questions "how far should we go to preserve them? Preserve them as what? As functional free-roaming herds or as deraci-

nated individuals in convenient roadside exhibits?"

We are guardians of the herds. The quality of their continued existence depends on the choices we make on their behalf — and anything we do or do not do will profoundly affect their destiny. We cannot truly let nature take its course. Nature employed predators to thin the herds and target animals that harbored disease, and the predators have been long gone, if they ever existed at all on East Coast barrier islands. We are unwilling to introduce wolves or mountain lions to control them, and we are unwilling to sit back and watch them starve when they outstrip their food sources. Intervention is the only humane option.

Maybe we should consider applying scientific management plans to ensure that they do not overwhelm their food sources or do irreparable damage to their environment. A multidisciplinary panel is optimally suited to making informed management decisions that balance environmental concerns, politics, public sentiment, and the needs of the horses themselves. The most compassionate option may be to allow them a wild existence within the limits set by researchers. This would involve curbing their fertility to restrict herd growth and restoring balance with the natural death rate, a balance once kept by natural predators.

The value of these feral horses would not be increased if we had documented proof of their origins or were somehow able to label them wild rather than feral. These horses should be preserved because of what they are. When we watch them grazing in the marshes or galloping like free spirits from the beach to the dunes, those of us with intact imaginations can feel the spirit of wildness well up in our own souls to run with the herd.

BEHAVIOR IN THE WILD

Horses are very sociable creatures and interact within established hierarchies.

Although the stallion is usually the dominant horse in the herd, in most free-roaming horse populations the lead mare makes the routine decisions, such as when and where the band will water, rest, or graze. When the herd travels, she often takes the lead. The stallion drives them from behind and keeps them together.

Horses communicate among themselves almost constantly, but the majority of these messages are non-verbal. Contrary to the almost continuous chorus of inappropriate whinnies and snorts dubbed into most Western movies, horses don't use their voices very often. Horses evolved to live on the grasslands, and herd members usually remain in sight of each other. The flattened ears and head toss of an irate mare is as effective as any vocalization and is unlikely to draw the attention of predators.

Pecking order is crucial to the social structure of the herd. When a new horse enters the band, fights ensue until the newcomer establishes a position in the hierarchy. After this initial trial, he or she generally maintains status by non-violent displays of threats such as pinning back the ears whenever another horse intrudes. These threats are well heeded by lower-ranking individuals; so actual kicking and biting are usually unnecessary. The purpose of a dominance system is to reduce overall aggression in the group, and as long as its position is well defined, a horse feels secure, even if very low in rank.

Social dynamics are usually more complicated than simple ranking. Horse number one may be dominant over horse number two, who is dominant over horse number three, while horse number three is dominant over horse number one. As confusing as these relationships can be to human researchers, every horse knows his or her status.

Age and size have something to do with which mares are dominant. Older mares tend to rise in social standing. The offspring of dominant mares tend to be higher in rank as well. Temperament is important. More belligerent horses rank higher. The stallion is not always the most dominant animal in the herd, especially if he is young and inexperienced.

Horses have personalities as unique and varied as those of dogs or people. Each forms friendships within the herd and displays unique preferences and quirks. A stallion may be affectionate with one mare and bicker constantly with another. Even mothering skills vary from mare to mare. Foals from previous years, especially fillies, may remain close to their mothers. A horse's basic need for companionship, a role or status within the herd, and physical contact with other horses contrast soberly with the unnatural, sterile lives of many domestic horses, kept solitary in a box stall or paddock much of the time.

Just as some gentlemen prefer blondes, some studs are attracted only to mares of a certain color, usually the color of his dam, and will even go so far as to collect a band of identically marked mares. Some stallions, both wild and domestic, will refuse to mate with mares of the "wrong" coat color. Most stallions prefer high-ranking mares and show little interest in fillies under the age of three, usually refusing to mate with their own daughters.

The rules are somewhat different for foals. Most of the time elders patiently tolerate a youngster's inquisitive peskiness, but when tempers flare, an impatient kick can be lethal to a foal. To circumvent this risk, foals adopt a posture similar to an exaggerated nursing position — neck and muzzle extended, ears

BONNIE S. URQUHART

Sexual behavior is core to the social organization of the herd.

153

out to the sides, with the corners of the mouth drawn back and jaw clapping, as if trying to chew a thick chunk of bubble gum. Steven Budiansky, in his excellent book *The Nature of Horses*, sees this as a ritualized version of a grooming gesture, similar to the posture a horse takes in mutual grooming activity. This gesture serves to shut off aggressive tendencies in mature horses. It translates to "don't hurt me, I'm only a little baby!"

Male foals are accepted and indulged by the herd for their first year or two. They can get away with outrageous behavior and social blunders and are regarded with affection by most members of the herd. They spend their days romping, wrestling, grazing, nursing, and sleeping. Life is good.

Usually around his second or third spring, the colt begins to feel the stir of hormones. Mares suddenly seem very interesting, and he is more inclined to assert his power. The harem stallion notices this, and sensing the evolution of a potential rival, loses patience. The stallion begins to harass the colt deliberately, initially not with overt aggression but by constantly picking on him, biting at the legs and neck in a less-than-friendly way, reminiscent of the way an employer would motivate an employee to quit so he would not have to fire him. If harassment doesn't send the colt off on his own, the stallion becomes more and more aggressive, sometimes inflicting deep bites that become infected. Biologist Ronald Keiper writes that on Assateague Island fifty-seven percent of the horses leave their natal band between the twelfth and twenty-fourth month.

The colts are usually bewildered by this aggression. After holding an established, secure spot in the social ranking for years, suddenly they are not wanted. Most of the time, they get the hint and reluctantly set out on their own. Horses are gregarious animals and are very uncomfortable without others of their own kind around. Evicted colts from the same natal band unite, and then group with those from other herds to form bachelor bands, usually of two to four individuals, transitional herds that will be their family for the next few years of their lives.

Bachelor bands do more than provide the adolescent colt with companionship. Through the frequent mock battles that make up much of their playtime, they learn the techniques necessary to defend a harem and win contests against other stallions. They shoulder and shove each other, mutually groom, and stand with their bodies touching, taking comfort from the physical contact. Between the ages of five and seven, the bachelor stud reaches full maturity and begins to steal mares from other stallions to form the nucleus of his own band.

Fillies are better tolerated by the stallion, but social pressure encourages three-quarters of them to leave their natal bands before puberty. Harem stallions are reluctant to mate with their own daughters. Mature males also generally prefer seasoned, experienced mares rather than shy maidens confused by the conflicting urges of adolescent heat cycles. Many fillies leave their bands to join others or to keep company with a bachelor stud, although she may wander alone for up to a year.

At other times, a mixed group of colts and fillies from the same band will stay together. These adolescent bands are temporary, and composition changes with time. As the colts mature into stallions, they depart one by one to form their own bands by stealing mares, until one stallion is left with the adolescent fillies, allowing him to develop a band with them as his foundation mares.

Typically, stallions are extremely attentive to newly acquired mares, nuzzling them, grooming them, and following them everywhere. They become the focus of the new stallion's whole existence, often a higher priority than even grazing. Young mares are likely to be happy in their new herds, but older mares often have strong bonds with one another and may attempt to return to their prior herds to rejoin their mare friends.

Band size is largest when a stallion is between the ages of nine and twelve, his prime years. Most bands range from eight to twelve animals, but Keiper reports a band as large as twenty-three.

Biologically, it would make little sense for stallions to fight bloody battles on a regular basis. Even fairly superficial wounds can cause lameness, infection, or even death. While stallions are capable of vicious warfare, they come to blows only as a last resort. Most of the power struggles between stallions from rival bands are resolved through ritualistic displays.

A confrontation between stallions usually begins with the two participants standing well apart from each other, watching each other intently. Each horse defecates, and each sniffs at the other's manure. Sometimes this alone somehow resolves the conflict.

If not, they arch their necks and each stud tries to look more formidable and powerful than the other. They approach each other, then jog side by side in an exaggerated trot known as a parallel prance. In these encounters, they appear to be sizing each other up, and if one is clearly less powerful or confident, the encounter ends as the subordinate stallion withdraws.

If the two stallions still feel equally matched, the ritual intensifies. The two rivals sniff at each other, especially at the muzzle and genitals and under the tail. Loud squeals and screams punctuate these investigations. The horse with the loudest, longest squeal often wins the conflict at this point.

If not, they begin to shove each other with their weight and bite at each other, especially at the legs. Pulling back, they rear and strike with the forelegs—this being more a display of power than a means of inflicting wounds, although by rearing and lunging, each can knock the opponent off balance. The fights can quickly turn ferocious. Back-kicking can inflict serious injury.

Stallion conflicts can last from a few minutes to the better part of an hour, the action taking place in rounds, or battles, separated by retreats to the band to graze. Eventually, one of the stallions will give up and take his band elsewhere.

When a stallion gets older and slower, a younger rival usually displaces him. The exiled stud really has no place to go. An old stallion, used to battling other males for most of his life, is not welcome in a bachelor herd. He can no longer steal mares. He is alone. Because of a horse's deep instinctive drive to be with other horses, this imposed isolation must be torture. Stress makes the outcast susceptible to disease. Most do not live more than a few more years.

Experienced stallions can often bluff their way through battles with younger, stronger rivals, retaining control of a herd into old age. Keiper writes of a twenty-one-year-old stud named Voodoo who kept a harem of seven mares and their foals despite his poor physical condition. Post-mortem examination revealed that his bottom incisors had been worn away so long before his death that the root spaces in his gums had actually healed over.

Courtship among horses is also ritualized. Each of the pair follows a set sequence of behaviors and responses. If the stallion is too hasty, he is likely to get bitten or kicked if he crowds a mare. A mare not fully in heat is unlikely to tolerate a stallion's sexual advances, so he is very careful to test her receptivity thoroughly before attempting to mate.

Before mating occurs, the stallion usually spends a lot of time near the mare, perhaps keeping her away from the rest of the band. She encourages his attentions by displaying signs of heat: frequent urination with raised tail, spraddled legs, and winking of the vulva. The stallion will thrust his muzzle into the puddle of urine, and perform flehmen — an odd-looking posture in which he stretches his neck up to full length, curls back his upper lip, and inhales deeply. It is thought that this posture allows the scent of the inhaled air to reach the vomeronasal organ, a specialized olfactory device designed to measure sex hormones and determine estrus.

When he sniffs into her nostrils, an equine greeting, she may squeal and strike out with one foreleg. The stallion readies her by licking and nibbling hindquarters, nuzzling and nudging, making nickering noises. The actual mating takes less than a minute. After copulation, the stallion often loses interest and resumes grazing.

Stallions are capable of mating year-round, but mares generally cycle only in the spring, summer, and early fall. Consequently, sexual interest declines in the fall and winter months.

The sexual instinct is present even among very young colts. Male foals test their mother's urine in the flehmen posture and ritualistically urinate over the puddle. Small male foals will attempt to mount other members of the herd — climbing aboard sideways or from the front most of the time, jumping on other male foals as well as fillies, herd mares, or their mothers or older sisters. This play behavior is eventually fine-tuned into adult sexual behavior.

In contrast, fillies do not display sexual behavior until their first heat cycles. A domestic filly usually shows heat as a yearling, but free-roaming horses tend to experience a later onset of puberty. Wild mares do not usually show mature sexual behavior or become pregnant before the age of three. Mature mares cycle every three weeks from about March through September if they are not pregnant. They come back into heat about seven to ten days after bearing a foal.

For a stallion during the breeding season, urination and defecation are almost always socially significant. Whenever one of his mares urinates, the herd stallion sniffs it, lifts his lip in the flehmen posture to determine her estrous status, and then urinates over the spot. Horses have an amazingly acute sense of smell, and scent-marking is one of the few ways they can leave messages for other horses that may happen by later. If another stallion encounters this spot, he would inevitably sniff the area and probably interpret the scent as "A mare was here, but she is claimed by this particular stallion." Marking is done more frequently if the mare is in heat, presumably to disguise the scent of her receptivity to other stallions.

Manure piles are often seen along well-traveled pony trails. Stallions stop and smell them thoroughly before depositing their own manure on the top of the heap. A horse can identify the scents of the other horses that used the pile, and apparently recognize their rank in the social hierarchy. So a manure pile serves as a sort of equine guest book of which stallions have recently passed. Keiper writes that stud piles on Assateague can grow to over six feet long and over two feet high.

Sources

In addition to the sources listed below, I used articles that appeared in the *Carteret County News-Times*, the *Island Breeze*, and *Equus, Coastwatch, Audubon*, and other magazines and newspapers, and materials in the collections at the Ocracoke Preservation Society, Carteret County Library, St. Marys Public Library, Tunxis Community College Library, and the Outer Banks History Center. The National Geographic Society and the Kentucky Horse Park supplied lots of very useful information. The following is organized by chapter, but some of the sources were instrumental to the writing of several chapters.

Chapter One: Wild Horses, Feral Horses

Darwin, Charles. *On the Origin of Species by Means of Natural Selection, or The Preservation of Favoured Races in the Struggle for Life*. London: John Murray, 1859.

Haines, Francis. *Horses In America*. New York: Thomas Crowell and Co., 1971.

Hunt, Kathleen. "Horse Evolution FAQ, v4.1, January 1993. http://www.talkorigins.org/faqs/horses.html.

Klinkenborg, Verlyn. "The Mustang Myth." *Audubon* (96, 1) January–February 1994.

Ryden, Hope. *America's Last Wild Horses*. New York: The Lyons Press, 2000.

Chapter Two: Where the Paved Road Ends

Chater, Melville. "Motor-Coaching through North Carolina." *National Geographic* 49, 5 (May 1926), 475–523.

Cothran, E. Gus. "The Banker Horse Genetic Research Program." Paper presented at the symposium Roanoke Decoded, Manteo, N.C., May 15, 1993.

Dolan, Robert, and Harry Lins. "The Outer Banks Of North Carolina." U.S. Geological Survey Professional Paper 1177-B. Washington, D.C.: Government Printing Office, 1993.

Dunbar, Gary S. *Historical Geography of the North Carolina Outer Banks*. Coastal Studies Series no. 3. Baton Rouge: Louisiana State University Press, 1958.

Frankenberg, Dirk. *The Nature of the Outer Banks*. Chapel Hill: University of North Carolina Press, 1995.

Thompson, Marye Ann. Personal letter from Spanish Mustang Registry, February, 1996.

Walsh, Jean. Letter to author from Spanish Barb Registry, February 1996.

Chapter Three: The Shifting Sands of Shackleford

Budiansky, Steven. *The Nature of Horses*. New York: The Free Press, 1997.

Draft Environmental Assessment of the Alternatives for

Managing the Feral Horse Herd on Shackleford Banks. Harkers Island, N.C.: Cape Lookout National Seashore, 1995.

Draft General Management Plan/Wilderness Study/Development Concept Plan, Cape Lookout National Seashore. Denver, Col.: National Park Service, May 1980.

General Management Plan/Development Concept Plan, Cape Lookout National Seashore. Denver, Col.: National Park Service, December 1982.

Jackson, Jaime. *The Natural Horse: Foundations for Natural Horsemanship.* Harrison, Ark.: Star Ridge Publishing, 1997.

Kirkpatrick, Jay. *Into the Wind: Wild Horses of North America.* Minocqua, Wis.: Northword Press, 1994.

Lenarz, Mark S. "Habitat Partitioning in Feral Horses: The Value of Being Dominant." Ecology 43 (01B) 1982.

North Carolina National Estuarine Research Management Plan. Raleigh: N.C. Division of Coastal Management, December 1990.

Rubenstein, Daniel. "Behavioral Ecology of Island Feral Horses." *Equine Veterinary Journal* 13 (1), 1981.

Rubenstein, Daniel, and Mace A. Hack. "Horse Signals: The Sounds and Scents of Fury." *Evolutionary Ecology* (6) 1992.

Ruffin, Edmund. "The Wild Horses, Their Qualities and Habits." In *Agricultural, Geological, and Descriptive Sketches of Lower North Carolina and the Similar Adjacent Lands*, 130–133. Raleigh: Privately printed, 1861.

Some Questions and Answers about the Horses at Rachel Carson. Raleigh: N.C. Division of Coastal Management.

Chapter Four: Bankers, Blackbeard, and Boy Scouts

Garber, Pat. *Ocracoke Wild.* Asheboro, N.C.: Down Home Press, 1995.

Henning, Jeanetta. *Conquistador's Legacy.* Ocracoke, N.C.: Privately printed, 1985.

"Spain in America." Supplement to *National Geographic* 181, 2 (February 1992).

Meader, Stephen W. *Wild Pony Island.* New York: Harcourt, Brace, 1959.

Newsome, A.R. "A Miscellany from the Thomas Henderson Letter Book, 1810–1811." *North Carolina Historical Review* 6, 4 (October 1929).

O'Neal, Rondthaler, Fletcher. *The Story of Ocracoke Island.* Marceline, Mo.: Walsworth Publishing and Charlotte, N.C.: Herb Eaton, Inc., 1976.

Chapter Five: Swimming the Channel and Chapter Six: Camping with Horses

Henry, Marguerite. *Misty of Chincoteague.* New York: Rand McNally, 1947.

Henry, Marguerite. *Stormy, Misty's Foal*. New York: Rand McNally, 1963.

Keiper, Ronald. *The Assateague Ponies*. Centreville, Md.: Tidewater Publishers, 1985.

Pleasants, Bernie. *Chincoteague Pony Tales*. Columbus, Ga.: Brentwood Christian Press, 1999.

Rodgers, R. Bruce. *Assateague Island National Seashore Feral Pony Management Plan*. U.S. National Park Service, 1985.

Wroten, William. *Assateague*. Centreville, Md.: Tidewater Publishers, 1985.

Vavra, Robert. *Such is the Real Nature of Horses*. New York: William Morrow and Company, 1979.

Chapter Seven: Horses of the Tropical Wilderness

Bratton, Susan, and Marlene Finly. *Horses of Cumberland Island*. U.S. National Park Service, 1995.

Draft Environmental Assessment: Alternatives for Managing the Feral Horse Herd on Cumberland Island National Seashore. St. Marys, Ga.: U.S. National Park Service, 6 March 1996.

Goodloe, R.A., R.J. Warren, E.G. Cothran, S.P. Bratton, and K.A. Trembicki. "Genetic Variation and its Management Applications in Eastern U.S. Feral Horses." *Journal of Wildlife Management* 55 (3), 1991.

Draft Plans and Environmental Impact Statement for Cumberland Island National Serashore. St. Marys, Ga.: U.S. National Park Service, December 14, 2000.

http://www.nps.gov/cuis/plan/

Acknowledgments

The experience of writing this book enriched my life in many ways. I learned a tremendous amount about horse behavior, and through untold hours spent following herds through marsh and dune gained a greater appreciation for the complexity of their apparently simple lives in the wild.

Many helpful and extraordinary people have earned my gratitude, and some have become close friends.

Jackie Duke, my editor at Eclipse Press, brought this project to fruition. I also am eternally indebted to John Bryans, editor-in-chief at Plexus Publishing. After trying for a year to fit my manuscript into his company's catalog, John forwarded it to Eclipse and remained supportive and helpful. Every contact I have had with John has left me feeling very good about the world.

Wynne Dough, former curator of the Outer Banks History Center, has been instrumental to the success of this project throughout the writing and editing process. He has an encyclopedic knowledge of historical matters and is an excellent writer and editor. His suggestions have improved my wording greatly, and he helped me revise and even co-wrote some of the historical paragraphs to ensure that this work maintains strict accuracy. He kept me motivated, and amazed me with the boundless energy he invested in this project.

The Corolla Wild Horse Fund provided some excellent information that helped me gain perspective on the plight of the Corolla herd. Members of this dedicated group have upended their lives to secure protection for these horses and should be applauded for that. The Foundation for Shackleford Horses has performed similar heroics in preserving the Cape Lookout National Seashore herd. Rick Ward, ranger at Assateague State Park, drove me all over the park and assisted me in many ways. He has also become a valued friend. Steve Yeomans and Dan Way filled me in on local lore when I visited Cedar Island in 1995, giving me fresh insight on the local herd while it still ran wild. Linda Scarborough, Ellen Cloud, and the others at the Ocracoke Preservation Society let me pore over and photocopy their fascinating scrapbooks.

I appreciate the cooperation of those who took the time to correspond with me and answer my many questions, including Dr. E. Gus Cothran, director of the Equine Blood Typing Laboratory at the University of Kentucky; Marye Anne Thompson, senior registrar of the Spanish Mustang Registry; Michael Rikard, resource manager of the Cape Lookout National Seashore; Dr. Phil Sponenberg of the Virginia Polytechnic Institute; Jean Walsh, Registrar of the Spanish Barb Breeder's Association; Carl Zimmerman, Chief of the Division of Resource Management, Assateague Island National Seashore; John Rutter of the National Geographic Society; and the Florida Cracker Horse Association.

Michael Levesque, my longtime friend, has helped me in incalculable ways. He sat for my children so I could conduct research, gave me books and software, and even drove me to North Carolina once when my own vehicle was too unreliable for long journeys. Skip Mudge, another longtime friend, likewise provided babysitting, encouragement, and transportation without complaint. Kim Davis is my sounding board and helps me sort out all that is important in life, from horses to kids. Alex Gruenberg proofread the final version and made valuable suggestions that improved readability. More important, Alex has been not only supportive but encouraging and inspiring as I tackle my various creative and academic pursuits.

My sister, Betsy Urquhart, regularly surfaced from writing her own book to keep my optimism intact with her cheerful and heartening notes. My mother, Joyce Urquhart, truly provided the lifeblood for this book — my creative juices flow directly from her inspiration.

My nursing professors at Southern Vermont College — Laurie Forfa, Barbara Waite, and Holly Madison — contributed significantly to this book by tightening my writing skills, honing my ability to do research, and holding me to high standards of accuracy. My coworkers on the maternal-child unit at St. Peters Hospital in Albany, New York, have been unflaggingly supportive, renewing my enthusiasm especially during the last grueling weeks of this project. They have been remarkably patient with the horse stories I bring to work and have always been interested in the progress of this project.

Finally, I wish to acknowledge my horse Fancy, my "recovering Psycho Pony." This amazing Connemara has the power to draw me out from behind the computer and restore balance to my life. He leaves his hoofprints in muddy pastures and on forest trails rather than in the sand, but he displays small flickers of an untamable aspect similar to that seen in wild horses. Not far beneath the veneer of domestication lurks the instinct and spirit of the original *Equus*. And thankfully, this spirit is contagious. When I am astride this noble animal galloping across a rippling meadow, he kindles the wildness in my own heart.

About the Author

BONNIE S. URQUHART

Bonnie S. Urquhart is a multifaceted person who only wishes that sleep were optional. Her years as a paramedic have taught her that nobody is promised a tomorrow, so she tries to milk every bit of life out of each moment. Urquhart thrives on learning and can get excited about a wide spectrum of topics, from physiology to horse-training techniques to rabbit coat-color genetics. She has authored articles in publications as dissimilar as *Equus* and the *American Journal of Nursing*. She often exhibits her award-winning artwork (her subjects are usually animals or children) and enjoys photography and Web design.

Skip Mudge

Horses have been her passion from infancy. She has been riding, training, teaching, and learning for decades, and she recently worked rehabilitating "hardluck" horses and teaching riding in Vermont. In her vanishing spare time Urquhart is enthusiastically learning dressage with her beloved Connemara, Fancy.

Urquhart was an urban paramedic for a decade and an emergency medical technician for years before that. She currently works as a registered nurse on a maternal-child unit. Urquhart is enrolled in the University of Pennsylvania's midwifery program and lives in Hershey, Pennsylvania.

Other Titles

from

ECLIPSE PRESS

A Division of The Blood-Horse, Inc.
PUBLISHERS SINCE 1916

THOROUGHBRED
Legends®
SERIES